CRASHING

CRASHING

CRASHING

CRASHING

CRASHING

CRASHING

CRASHING

CRASHING

CRASHING

CRASHING

CRASHING

CRASHING WITHOUT BURNING
(LIFE AFTER FAILURE)

Crashing Without Burning
Life After Failure

C. David Matthews

PEAKE ROAD
Macon, Georgia

ISBN 1-57312-155-X

Crashing Without Burning
Life After Failure

C. David Matthews

Copyright © 1997

Peake Road
6316 Peake Road
Macon, Georgia 31210-3960
1-800-747-3016

Library of Congress Cataloging-in-Publication

Matthews, C. David.
        Crashing without burning: life after failure/
        C. David Matthews.
        x + 118 pp.   6" x 9" (15 x 23 cm.)
        Includes bibliographical references.
        ISBN 1-57312-155-X   (alk. paper)
        1. Failure (Christian theology).
        2. Loss (Psychology)—Religious aspects—Christianity.
        I. Title.
        BT730.5.M38   1997
        248.8'6—dc21   97-8705
                                                        CIP

Contents

Preface vii

Living in the Ruins

1 When Bad Things Are *Done* by Good People 3
2 God Who Lets Us Fail 13
3 Exorcising the Past 17
4 Surviving Exile 29

Rethinking the World

5 The Environment of Failure 39
6 "The Vale of Soul Making" 47
7 What Cannot Be Shaken 51
8 The Size and Shape of Truth 57
9 Learning to Pray 65

The Inner Promised Land

10 Light in Failure's Night 75
11 The Great Invitation 83
12 Faith for the Journey 91
13 The Gift of Adequacy 99
14 Seeing Beyond Our Living 107

Preface

Failure is a form of death. Something is lost, often something so valuable that a person's life is changed forever. What makes failure different from most other forms of death is the sense, justified or not, of personal responsibility. Therefore, the human reaction to failure usually produces the blended bitterness of guilt and grief. These can be key ingredients in creating despair, or they can become redemptive material for the making of a new and better life.

I am a survivor of the kind of moral crisis that has destroyed many pastoral careers and secular ones as well. The scenario is so familiar as to be relatively uninteresting—a sign of the times. Nearly twelve years ago, and after ten years as the senior minister of a large church, my affair with a fellow church member was discovered and made public. The devastation was far-reaching, and many other people suffered because of my sin. The cost to me was my ministry in that church, my marriage, the extramarital relationship, and much of the rest of my world of people, places, and things. Since that shattering experience, survival and the long process of rebuilding have required most of my energies.

This is not a book I ever expected to write. Our lives tend to stray from the scripts we have prepared, and can become either wonderfully or frightfully extemporaneous. Rip Van Winkle was not the first or last sleeper to awaken in unanticipated surroundings. In real life we usually also wake up to the realization that we are either partially or primarily responsible for the creation of this different world. Suddenly there is the necessity of rewriting the script, beginning with a premise we might not have chosen. In the netherworld of failure, this is life's most difficult task.

This book is about that task. I have written it with one reservation that deserves mentioning. A clear sign of our culture's decline is that we have not only developed a taste for other people's blood, but are also willing to sell our own. Having lost a transcendent orientation, we have no vital sense of depth, so we have turned in horizontal directions for the satisfaction of our need for meaning. We fashion celebrity idols, grant them dominion over our lives, then smash them when the gilding starts to peel. We construct a glittering world of appearances that, when it is found to be hollow, we redo with cosmetic surgery, believing that, if we can only keep it looking good, this vast emptiness will nourish us.

This is what make us such "peeping toms." We keep thinking that inside someone else's life is the treasure we seek. Our appetite for the dark sides and private lives of famous people is insatiable. Media merchants are only feeding us what we want. Even in the "Christian" market sensationalism sells. The average Christian is as enamored with our superficial culture as anyone else. Evil is glamorized in the process of being opposed, and the "born again" life of a quick-fix gospel is recommended in much the same seductive way.

I do not want to use my mistakes either to titillate or to elicit the kind of sympathy that would make me the veiled hero of my own story. I hope the book itself will make clear that my purpose is something larger and more important than writing about myself. A decade of dealing with the inside and outside of moral failure is not long enough for me to speak glibly about it.

Finally, three gardens grow in my life, each overlapping the others in a blessed trinity. One is my faith, which has scorch marks on the gate and reinforced places along the fence, but which grows with deeper roots beneath more delicate blossoms. Grace not only did not forsake me, but has allowed me, after a long, dark night, to continue what I have always known was my calling. Not a few caretakers kept their hands in my dry soil until I could resume my own gardening. My inner life still needs weeding, but it is an ever-more peaceful place to be, and most days my work and my worship are one.

The second garden is my family: especially Priscilla, a most splendid companion; my children who are inexhaustible sources of amazement, consolation, and joy; and my brothers and sisters, only one by blood and the rest by spirit, who have loved me in my brokenness as if I were whole.

The third garden is the church, the community of faith, which I have learned I need whether it needs me or not, and which I find happens best in some of the smallest and most unlikely places. Life is not the same, but life is good.

My hope is to speak redemptively to some of the things those who have experienced serious failure have in common. I have crashed, but I have not burned. I know the devastation of personal failure, but I can speak of life beyond failure. In recent years I have found that these two credentials provide access into some places where I have not been welcomed before and where I have not been particularly eager to go. My official sphere of ministry may be smaller, but the world of fellow failures and strugglers is larger than I realized, and so is the word of hope I am privileged both to hear and to proclaim.

> *O human race! Born to ascend on wings,*
> *Why do ye fall at such a little wind?*
>
> —Dante
> *The Divine Comedy*

> *The vessel he was making of clay was spoiled in the potter's hand, and he reworked it into another vessel, as seemed good to him.*
>
> —Jeremiah 18:4

Living in the Ruins

Not, I'll not, carrion comfort, Despair, not
    feast on thee;
Not untwist—slack they may be—these last
    strands of man
In me or, most weary, cry I can no more. I
    can;
Can something, hope, wish day come, not
    choose not to be.

—Gerard Manley Hopkins
    "Carrion Comfort"

1

When Bad Things Are *Done* by Good People

The phone call comes that you had almost stopped fearing. It is like a detonation at your core, a silent subterranean explosion that pushes your brain against your skull so that you feel your head will burst. You have been discovered. Your long, unblinking vigilance has not been enough. Your secret is out, out of your control and all possibility of containment. As pervasive as smoke, it will leave a dark film and a charred smell on everything.

Your mind resists the intrusion. Surges of adrenaline prepare you for flight. There is nowhere to go. Maybe if you are very still the horror will go away. It will not. You fight panic, avoid falling, manage to stand and walk out of the room. "I need to be away for awhile." You get through the hall without seeing anyone and are out of the building. Outside, the world that will never be the same for you ambles on, oblivious to the pall that has fallen all around it.

In all the considered scenarios of possible discovery, all the inventories of potential consequences, you never imagined such a sense of doom. You begin visualizing the stricken faces of the people you love, and you can hardly breathe. The rationalizations you have used to reinforce your private world crumble and vanish, and you are left with what you should have known: there is no excuse.

You begin formulating survival strategies for the next few hours. You can conceive of no future beyond that. How could you let it come to this? Why did you not anticipate it? Where are your preparations for so predictable a disaster?

This dark drama will have many episodes, but its bleak plot will be unrelieved. You will struggle daily toward distant lights, fight to keep your hope up, and lie down at night exhausted by an existence that goes nowhere but does not end. You will feel banished from your own history. You will grieve over the loss of whatever status you may have had as a good person. And the worst part of the long judgment you must endure will be the terrible knowledge that you have no one to blame but yourself.

Power Failure and Moral Failure

Failure is the death of an intention. It may be our own or the expectations others have for us, but failure, by definition, is a missed target.

All failures are not the same, however, either in their nature or their significance. Most failures fall into the category of what might be called "power failure." This is when some intention is simply beyond my powers to fulfill. It may be because the intention was too idealistic in its conception, as when I announced in first grade that I wanted to be President of the United States and couldn't understand what was so funny. It may be because of intervening circumstances, or miscalculations, or factors impossible to anticipate, but power failure occurs when, for whatever reason, I find my human capacities inadequate in relation to some intention.

I remember Kyle's first circus. I was prepared for my son to be mesmerized by trapeze artists, balancing acts, and lion tamers. At one point, after a hundred-feet-high triple somersault or something, when my own palms were sweating, I turned to Kyle and exclaimed, "Can you believe that?" With steady conviction he replied, "I can do that." Nothing happened at the circus that day that Kyle was not certain he could do. What were we growing here—Norman Vincent Peale? Later that same day, however, our backyard became an arena of painful reality for this imaginative little boy. My son has excelled in many things over the years since, but as circus material he remains a failure.

Power failures are not always expressions of physical limitations. For instance, I may find at mid-passage that I no longer have the heart for some ventures, having simply lost interest or having moved on to other things. This, too, is a form of power failure, although less significant, because I now lack the desire or will to finish what I started.

Power failures may or may not be demoralizing and life-changing. In this they run the gamut from barely noticeable blips on the screen of daily life to screen-shattering tragedies. If I run out of daylight before I get Saturday's chores done, that failure will not bring on Armageddon. On the other hand, if I fail to qualify for some career advancement, it may affect where my kids go to college, or if they do, and whether I retire to a Greek isle or to my den.

There is another category of failure. It is more serious and more expressive of our unique human nature. It is moral failure. Moral failure involves a decision. When I make a decision that violates an intention I have in some way acknowledged to have moral significance, this is a moral failure. It is not a lack of power, but the willful misuse of power. It is moral precisely because I have the power to fulfill a good intention and choose not to.

Life as distinctively human is comprised of covenants, that is, mutual commitments. Vows at an altar, treaty signings, handshakes, contracts, appointments, laws, ordinances, hugs—all are for sealing and clarifying covenants. They make our intentions morally binding. Decisions that violate covenants are moral failures.

Moral failures come in all sizes, but always represent betrayal. If I cheat on my diet, my wife, my employer, or the speed limit, I have made a choice that constitutes infidelity. I have broken a covenant.

My power failures, of course, can result in suffering, either my own or that of someone else, as when a family cannot get to the hospital in time to save one of its members. Power failures can affect and change our lives, but they do not necessarily diminish our souls. A moral failure, in addition to whatever else it does, diminishes me. Moral failure invariably produces alienation, either within the self or between one's self and others. It is destructive to one's personhood and to one's relationships because something or someone has been betrayed. Betrayal is not the result of limited powers; it is a choice.

A distinction between these two kinds of failure is critical. One sign of a sick culture is the blurring of this distinction, so that one of these two categories is absorbed into the other. For example, in a culture in which success is the supreme virtue, failure is the unpardonable sin. In other words, where quantitative success is God, power failure is an obscenity and will be treated with the seriousness of moral failure. Those who fail in any way will suffer banishment, one way or another. This is why we pressure ourselves and our children to succeed, regardless of the pursuit. Better a successful automaton than a failed artist.

On the other hand, in a culture in which the secular and the scientific gradually displace all forms of spiritual orientation, any instance of failure may come to be treated as merely power failure. People are not evil; they are sick. They are not immoral; they are immature.

Our full humanity depends on keeping the distinction clear. Power failure is technically a witness to our finitude only and should be accepted as an expression of natural human limitations. Moral failure, however, reflects our essentially spiritual nature and our capacity for irresponsible behavior and destructive choices.

The Principle of Ambiguity

Rabbi Kushner, author of *When Bad Things Happen to Good People*, gives helpful wisdom on the mysteries of external evil and innocent suffering. As unavoidable as these perplexing issues are, even more obstinate and disturbing are the mysteries of internal evil. What does it mean when bad things are *done* by good people?

We have all known the shock of discovering that someone we thought we knew has done something we can hardly believe. When she decided you were old enough, your most mischievous aunt let you in on a family secret. Great-uncle Andy once killed a man and spent some time in prison. Of course, it was a long time ago, when he was young, and nobody ever talks about it, but she was sure it had actually happened. There had been a fight over something, and when it was over, the other man was dead. Uncle Andy was charged with second-degree murder and did time in the penitentiary at Rusk.

You could not quit thinking about it. This piece of information had raised a curtain on the adult world. Here was color, intrigue, and passion that you had never imagined. You had always seen this assemblage of older kin one-dimensionally, as good, God-fearing, and simple. The life you envisioned for them beyond family reunions was too boring to even think about. In this new light they took on flesh and a full range of real feelings. They became interesting, even fascinating, with their mysterious pasts. They also became less safe, a bit threatening. Who was this man who knew what it felt like to kill another human being? What else had he done or thought of doing? What other dark secrets were buried in your family's history? What began as titillation became a bit troubling. A chunk of your innocence had been knocked off. It would never again be as easy to differentiate between good people and bad people.

The other side of the graying of your world you experienced with the mother of a schoolmate. The first time you went to

Tim's house you were put off by everything. It was a messy environment, prioritizing the comfort of those who lived there. Everything was not in its proper place. Tim's mother did not look like a mother. She wore bright red lipstick. She smoked. She was casual in everything. And, worst of all, she was divorced from Tim's father, and this was Texas in 1950. You did not tell your mother about Tim's mother.

Across a school year, however, Tim's house became a special place to you, and his mother a growing enigma. She continued to break your mother-mold, but she became your friend. Unlike most adults, she made eye contact with you and listened when she asked you a question. Then, in the spring, she and Tim came to your piano recital, and a few days later you got a little note in the mail from her saying you were headed for Carnegie Hall. You had nowhere to put Tim's mom in the light and dark categories of your mind. It is not just confusing; it is painful to have people enter your life for whom you have built no rooms.

The greater confusion and deeper pain, however, was the increasing discovery within yourself of realities for which you found no convenient accommodation. Your child-self, pronounced good both by your Creator and your procreators, turned out to have a basement full of incorrigible selves. You did your best to keep the cellar door shut, but they banged on it incessantly and frequently threatened to blow things up.

You found yourself more and more in conflict with yourself, which made for interesting competition. You felt like a contradiction and found yourself saying, "I can't believe I did that!" or, "What was I thinking about when I said that?" You often wondered in private whether you were a good person or a bad person.

The seminary I attended has never been considered a monument to theological subtleties. In fact, it has specialized more in evangelistic fervor than intellectual ferment. It is not where you would look for a Niebuhr or a Tillich. But truth is subversive, and I found these two great theologians there. They taught me the second most important thing I know about God and the world. The first, by the way, is that the sovereign and holy reality of God is both more profound and more mysterious than our worthiest concepts.

In my first class in systematic theology I was assigned a content book report on the first volume of Reinhold Niebuhr's *The Nature and Destiny of Man*. It caught me at a desperately teachable moment and threw open all my windows and doors. I breathed fresh air. I saw that good and bad are not separate hemispheres but are present and intermingled in all things, save God alone. Am I a good person or a bad person? Neither. Both. My glory is that I am, though finite, created in the image of God. My misery is that I am a sinner. Both are true to my human reality, and they intertwine in me in a genuine paradox. This knowledge can save me from exalted expectations of myself if I accept that I am a sinner, and from despair if I accept that I am made in the image of God. God is the only absolute. All else, including me, is ambiguous.

In 1963, Henry Luce invited Paul Tillich to speak at the fortieth anniversary celebration of *Time* magazine. The site was the Waldorf Astoria in New York City. The audience included 284 subjects of *Time* cover stories. Tillich sat on the dais next to Adlai Stevenson, not far from Douglas MacArthur. In that rarified company he spoke on the human condition. He insisted that it is consistently ambiguous, an "inseparable mixture of good and evil, of creative and destructive forces." At both the individual and social levels "there is nothing unambiguously creative and nothing unambiguously destructive. They accompany each other inseparably."[1]

This perspective is fortification against disillusionment because it discourages idolatry of all kinds. Only God is perfectly good, completely true. All else exists in the co-mingling gray of ambiguity and paradox. No person, no institution, no nation, no ideology, no created thing is deserving of our absolute, uncritical allegiance. God only is pure light, in whom alone there is no "shadow of turning" (Jas 1:17, KJV).

Surprise Endings

When "bad" things are done by "good" people . . .

- It demonstrates the essential ambiguity of every human being.
- It confirms the biblical perspective that sin is universal and paradoxical.
- It underscores the mysterious complexity of motives, circumstances, and emotions behind every human act.
- It is a reminder than I am capable of more evil than I may realize, and, therefore, must manage my life conscientiously and reverently.
- It is not necessarily the end of the world.

The Bible is full of surprises, which people discover when they actually read it, which doesn't happen very often. Looking for a safe place to hide your valuables? Try the book of Nahum in the Old Testament. No one will ever look there. An obvious sign, though few see it, of our propensity for idolatry is the way we make the Bible an object of worship instead of a guide to faith. Fetishism lives.

Unstick the pages and you will find that the "Good Book" has a serious shortage of good people. There is one, but he himself attributed goodness only to God, as a genuinely good person would. The rest look like us. They are moral and spiritual mongrels, possessing in their depths all the light and darkness of the cosmos, stretched to near-breaking by the polarities of their opposite possibilities, and confounded by their own zigzagging between grandeur and shame.

They are not remembered primarily for any goodness they possessed. Most are remembered for their failure, but their failure in relation to God's goodness. They are remembered for the surprise endings the recreative power of grace fashioned out of their failures.

Is it possible, when judgment falls like a collapsing building, that survival is not the only question? Is there a journey toward one's true self that begins in the wreckage of some failed intention? Can failure, even moral failure, be creative? When bad things are done by good people, is it the end or a beginning?

Note

[1]Wilhelm and Marion Pauck, Paul Tillich: His Life and Thought, Vol. 1: Life (New York: Harper & Row, 1976) 273-74.

2

God Who Lets Us Fail

A young woman is home for a visit. She doesn't get home as much as she would like, so there is a lot of catching up to do. She and her mother are in the kitchen talking as they work together on a meal.

"Mother, I think he loves me."

"Oh? Why do you think so?"

"Because he wants to be with me all the time. Because he cares about the little things in my life. Back when I sprained my ankle, he wouldn't let me do anything. He went to the store for me. He cleaned my apartment. He even cooked some. But he's like that all the time. He is so attentive, he's sometimes funny. I just think he loves me because of all the things he does for me."

"Well, that's wonderful, honey. It certainly sounds like he loves you."

It does. The test of love, we know, is involvement. We measure the degree of love by the extent of the involvement. I know there is something wrong if you say you love me but never come around or call, never share any of my concerns, never do anything for me. On the other hand, even if you cannot or do not tell me you love me, I may know that you do because of the ways you are involved in my life.

What about God? Does God love us? Sometimes, frankly, God does not seem to pass love's test of involvement. Our days pass routinely. We work, we rest, we play, we struggle. There is good news, bad news, no news. Some things work out; some things don't. Where is God in all of this?

I once bought a book because I was intrigued by its title, but then I forgot to read it. (Probably I'm not alone.) Several years later I finally read Geddes MacGregor's *He Who Lets Us Be: A Theology of Love.* It helped me relate some lessons I was learning as a parent to the ongoing work of understanding God. For example, while one measure of love is the extent of involvement, sometimes love's test is the degree of restraint.

Jesus, who called God "Father," once told a story about a father who possessed great love and profound wisdom. One of his sons got lost in a far country in quest of the good life. The other got lost at home, which is easier to do. The father waited. Eventually one of the sons came back to him, and it was as if the boy had come back from the dead. We don't know what the other son did. The story is left for us to finish. But the father is a perfect model of love that waits.

It takes mature love to endure the pain of restraint, of letting go, or letting be. The easier thing, by far, is to act, to coerce, to take control.

During the first years of a child's life, parental love must be expressed in intense and constant involvement. An infant is helpless, absolutely dependent. Literally everything must be done for a baby. Soon, however, the long process of weaning must begin, and good parenting means gradually giving your children away. This is the only way a child can grow into a responsible self. It is wise love that knows when to move in and when to step back.

From the "wean-ee" side of this transaction "wean-ers" must seem heartless and cruel. They take training wheels off of bicycles, and their children run into trees and hit the pavement with soft little elbows and knees. They say, "I think you're ready," and get out of the car, leaving the operation of the most dangerous piece of machinery in the world in the hands of a teenager, the most dangerous person in the world! They get mail from college hinting that something green would be nice, and they send back brownies. What a pain!

The deeper pain is the parent's in restraining, letting go, letting be. The French have a proverb: *Aimer est souffrir*, "to love is to suffer." The great risk in letting be is that it might mean letting fail. This is what keeps parents awake nights. The world into which the child goes looks like a mine field. Anything could happen.

Do you remember the little bird you found once? It would have died if you hadn't found it. Your parents let you keep it. You named it, nursed it, protected it, and watched it grow. You got very close to that little bird. It was hard to face the day when you had to let it go. How could you do it? Only one way. The caring that made it difficult made it possible. Your parents had explained that the bird was made for a larger world than a box. You asked, "But what if something happens to it?" They said, "That's the risk you must take. If you keep it, it will die for sure, and it will never become what it was meant to be." In a costly act of caring, with anxious mind and heavy heart, you let it go.

Who can say with accuracy when God's love is expressed through direct involvement in our lives and when it is manifested in restraint? Beware of those who think they can. To claim that God is love, however, is surely to attribute to God both the power of restraint and the capacity for suffering.

On my office door I have a rough little wooden cross I bought in Sante Fe, New Mexico. I need it at that threshold of my daily life. It reminds me in my coming and going that there is a cross in the heart of God who lets me fail and weeps when I do

3

Exorcising the Past

The demons that most bedevil our lives reside, not in the here and now, but in the past and the future. It has been suggested that the reason children live so fully in the present is that they have no vital sense of the past or the future. They live in a timeless now. Adults, on the other hand, are often so preoccupied with the past and future that the present ceases to exist. Adulthood involves high susceptibility to the diseases of time. Anxiety, fear, guilt, and grief may have many secondary causes, but basically they are disabilities with regard to past time and future time.

Someone in the immediate aftermath of significant failure will experience a heightened sensitivity to time that approaches burn levels. The past becomes a looming tyranny threatening to devour the future, and seconds pound like an anvil in your chest. The urge to disappear into the vortex swirling at one's center is of course to be resisted, but also the tendency to isolate oneself from all others. Following failure, this tendency is frequently facilitated by the fact that people are already running in the opposite direction at warp speed. We are so afraid of failure, we take no chances that it might be contagious.

Before the failure event has slipped beyond the immediate past, we will need to talk about it, whether we want to or not. Just anyone will not do for the high, holy work of hearing. Just any professional listener will not do any more than just any religious person. Our priests must be chosen carefully. There are sheep shearers out there in shepherds' clothing and emotional vampires among our closest acquaintances. There is also a trustworthy, caring, competent someone. God's true priests have infiltrated everywhere, usually not looking the part and sometimes not knowing themselves who they are. While the pain is fresh, it needs to be shared with whatever compassionate other a gracious providence has brought within reach. Unshared pain is a poison.

Even when responsibly shared, the pain of failure leads to certain natural and predictable reactions. Not to experience these at all would reveal us as less than human. Therefore, negative as they seem, they are signs of our higher nature.

Failure always results in the loss of something, even if it is only psychological or emotional, like a goal or a self-image. The natural response to loss is grief. We grieve over the loss of things as significant as our loved ones and as (relatively) insignificant as our hair.

Grief works in partnership with guilt. Sometimes one takes the lead, sometimes the other, but neither tends to do business with us alone.

If we have only suffered a power failure, guilt feelings are technically inappropriate. Power failures, as such, are an expression of our finitude, the limits of which are not our responsibility, since we did not create ourselves. The psyche seldom gets this message, however, and every experience of grief is interlaced to some degree with feelings of guilt, whether they are appropriate or not.

Likewise, guilt feelings are always interspersed with grief. In moral failure the unique ingredient is personal responsibility; therefore, guilt feelings are appropriate. Moral failure not only means that something has been done, however, but also that something has been lost. It may be a sense of innocence, or it may be most of one's entire world, but it is loss. The fact that we are the culprits does not keep us from grieving over what we lose.

The point is that in all human failure, guilt and grief, in varying combinations, are part of the emotional price we pay. To the extent that they are simply locked in the basement or buried alive in some tomb of denial, they become demonic parasites that drain their host without mercy. This is failure leading to spiritual death. Fortunately, there is a better way.

Guilt: Shame or Regret?

I threw the rock. I have never been able to throw anything that accurately since.

It was Wichita Falls, Texas, in the 1940s, a world away. I can't remember much about the setting or the event itself. I can't remember who the big kid was or what the two of us had been doing. I haven't a clue what I was wearing or how I looked. But the emotions I experienced after that terrible event I not only remember but can replay up and down my central system. Those feelings are as real to me as if the event had just happened.

My parents and I were visiting my grandparents, as we did several times a year. This older boy lived in the same block. I was impressed with him, since older was better. I desperately wanted him to be impressed with me. One afternoon we were sitting on the curb watching the cars go by. He produced a rock and said, "I'll bet you wouldn't throw this rock at one of those cars." I didn't say anything. "You wouldn't do it," he said, "because you know you couldn't hit it."

Call me a sucker, but a short while later I was standing behind a tree, out of sight of the passing cars, with this rock in my hand. I waited for one that was going pretty slow and just as it got even with me, I threw the rock.

I remember that, as I threw it, I didn't know whether to hope I would hit it or miss it. I hit it. The rock hit the little vent window that used to be a part of car windows. It only cracked the window, but it sounded to me like a huge chandelier falling on a stone floor.

19

I freaked. I couldn't believe what I had done. The big kid was gone. The car stopped. I ran as if wild dogs were at my heels. I could not stop running. When I reached another time zone, I decided it was safe to slow down.

By a circuitous route I made my way back to my grandparents' house. I went in the back door and, with what I thought was sufficiently calm demeanor, told my mother that I was going to lie down for a little while.

The little day bed on which I slept when we visited there became my rack of torture. I felt like I was inventing anxiety. I knew that at any moment the doorbell would ring, and my eternal damnation would begin.

The cynic will ask if it was guilt that consumed me or just the fear of getting caught. I do not know. In the existential moment, it hardly matters, and I become cynical around people who think they can find a line between those two states of mind.

The doorbell never rang.

I've chosen an anecdote from as long ago as the 1940s and as far away as Wichita Falls, Texas, to protect myself both from your judgment and from legal liability. But I could document the point with many more recent examples. The point? There is guilt in all of us.

Whether it is justified or not, the sense of guilt is deeper in us than we know. It reaches considerably below the sins we can remember and confess. It plunges into the bottomless regions of the unconscious and terrorizes aspects of the self that the conscious mind cannot reach, much less control. This subterranean sense of guilt, the psychoanalysts and the theologians agree, is one of the marks of our humanity.

Some inner voice has always whispered, "Someone must pay." Ancient people offered up their firstborn, tribal people mutilated their own bodies, and in Israel, the great temple housed an elaborate system of sacrifice because someone must pay. Today we accept more stress than we can bear, tighten tender muscles into hard knots of pain, and develop myriad diseases because someone must pay. We become stoop-shouldered or develop chronic back pain from carrying some burden of guilt, like the mother who punishes herself forever because of her child's birth defect despite the fact that she was in no sense responsible for it.

This sense of guilt waits to pounce with its great weight on any misdemeanor that enters the field of the conscious mind's vision. Give this demon something specific to gnaw on, and it will not relent.

The most important question about guilt is: What does it become? In most of us, it becomes either shame or regret.

Shame is the result of not only taking responsibility for what I have done, but of letting that failure play a lead role in defining or confirming my sense of my identity. Shame makes no distinction between what I have done and who I am.

Dogs are great. God created dogs so that we could learn to laugh at ourselves without going to the psychiatrist. Dogs, unless somewhere along the way they have been influenced by cats (and you know which dogs I mean), are more devoted to us than we are to ourselves. Whatever we tell them, they believe. Dogs invented tail wagging and licking because they believe us when we say, "Good dog!" Dogs also invented groveling as a way of letting us know they believe us when we say, "Bad dog!" Shame is when we act like dogs.

Regret, on the other hand, is the result of taking responsibility for what I have done, but of refusing to see my failure as a final verdict on who I am. I regret what I have done, but it is not the defining moment of my personhood.

What determines whether our guilt becomes shame or regret? The difference is whether we believe the last word on guilt is a word of condemnation or a word of grace.

I serve the church joyfully and gratefully, but I am glad the church does not have the last word on my guilt. Too often the church has only compounded the problem, acting as if its purpose is to induce guilt feelings.

At some point in my life I was overtaken by what has been called "the romance of preaching." Therefore, I detest what preaching has come to mean in daily speech. When someone is berating us, we say, "Quit preaching!" A church member told me once that if he didn't feel guilty on Sunday afternoon, he didn't feel like he had been to church. Thank God preachers don't have the last word on our guilt. God does. It has already been uttered. And it is not a word of condemnation.

According to the Gospel of Luke, the first of the last words of the dying Jesus were, "Father, forgive them, for they do not know what they are doing." Can you imagine that? Most victims go down cursing their assailants. Here is one who prays for his executioners' forgiveness as he is being executed.

Christians have always taken forgiveness seriously. We believe God forgives sin. Sometimes we even believe we ought to forgive each other! But we have always known that forgiveness has a prerequisite: repentance. Forgiveness is preceded by repentance. We would expect Jesus to forgive his Jewish and Roman antagonists after a proper repentance. But on Jesus' dying day forgiveness preceded repentance.

Isn't it true, after all, that grace always motivates better repenting than condemnation? Condemn me, and I may never repent. I can be awfully stubborn when being accused. But with accepting love you can open the gates of my mind and my mouth, paving the way for my confession.

I threw the rock. The doorbell never rang. But my mother knew. She knew something was wrong. I could never figure that out. How did she know? I thought maybe God told her.

After giving me about all the writhing time I could stand, she came in and sat on the bed. "What's wrong?" she asked. I tried to say nothing was wrong, but it was no use. It all came gushing out—all of it, a full confession. And what a relief! What incredible relief!

Mother didn't let me off the hook. God doesn't either. But before I went to bed that night, we had settled it. I knew that

everything was basically ok. Even if that doorbell rang, everything was ok.

Grief into Gratitude

Practical people, who are in the majority and whom I envy, like
things clearly defined, goal-oriented, and organized into steps.
So, where are they when the assembly instructions are being
written for the things we buy?

When I was young and thought I was clever, I preached a
sermon entitled "Seven Steps to Successful Hypocrisy." With
sarcasm unencumbered by subtlety, I said that since we seem
determined to be hypocrites, and since success is our culture's
highest good, I was providing practical help for becoming the
most successful hypocrite possible.

The service was broadcast locally on the radio. A listener in
one of the nursing homes tuned in late, just as I was saying:
"Step Three: Never pray except in public." She called me that
afternoon to say that she had hoped never to live so long as to
hear what she heard that morning and that if I was going to
work for the devil, I ought to have the decency to admit it.

Undeterred, I am now offering practical suggestions for living through the grief, or guilt-grief complex, that inevitably
follows failure. I will attempt to avoid both sarcasm and
subtlety.

Hang On. Sometimes we just have to hang on. In every storm
there is the moment of greatest intensity. Usually it does not last
very long. While it lasts, the best thing to do, and maybe the
only thing, is to hang on.

Things change. For better or for worse, nothing remains the
same. In the first crush of grief we often must simply find a way
to endure until the external and internal landscapes begin to
change. They will. Changes impossible to see or imagine are in
everybody's future.

Accept Your Feelings. My mind and body find it difficult to believe that anything that hurts is normal. When I return to the YMCA after one of my frequent fitness sabbaticals, that friendly place has become a house of pain. After a few minutes on the treadmill, my body begins to send emergency signals to my brain: "Red alert! Abandon mission! Report to ER!"

A part of dealing with grief is accepting it as natural and normal. Of course there is abnormal, neurotic grief, grief that needs professional attention. Usually, however, grieving over a loss is as natural as laughing at a joke. It helps if someone says to me, "Of course, you feel like that. That's the way you're supposed to feel, given what you've been through." Whether they do or not, I must say it to myself. My feelings are a given. How I respond to my feelings is a variable. Realistic acceptance of my feelings is the first step in a healthy response.

Interpret Your Feelings. Grief is a testimony to love. There is no grief where there is no love. We do not grieve just because something has been lost. We grieve because something or someone we love has been lost. It may be an inappropriate love that has us weeping, or even a destructive love, but grieving is the downside of loving.

Against the black backdrop of fresh loss this truth may seem dim consolation. However, it can be a seed of reassurance for those times that border on despair when we question everything meaningful in the world and everything noble in ourselves. If we can understand that what we experience as negative (grief or guilt) is rooted in something positive (our capacities for love and for goodness), we will have begun laying a foundation for recovery and growth.

Trust God. Come to me in my despondency with the suggestion that I trust in God, and you are likely to get a weak reaction. Pious admonitions tend to sound trite and hollow to me even when I am in good shape. But when I am depressed they sound almost cruel. However, things become trite because

24

they possess, or did at one time, some element of truth. The truth is, I need to trust in God, especially when I have experienced significant loss.

Every day at Walt Disney World one thousand items are lost. I have never been to Mickey's Lost and Found, but it must the size of Space Mountain. The point is, someone has to *find* one thousand lost items for us to have the statistic. Lost, then, is a relative term.

Paleontologist Teilhard de Chardin wrote of the "fruit" of his life being "received up into One who is eternal," of knowing "that the best of me passes on forever into One who is more beautiful and greater than I."[1] St. Paul offers a doxology in his epistle to the Romans that praises God as the Source, Guide, and Goal of all things: "For from him and through him and to him are all things" (Rom 11:36). People's concepts of the eternal realm differ greatly, but are they not all a way of affirming that in God nothing of value is ever truly lost?

Trusting God in our grief does not mean deluding ourselves with a false hope of recovering what has been lost. It is more a matter of believing that what is lost to us is somehow kept by the One in whom all things exist, and, therefore, it is not ultimately lost at all.

Trust the Process. "Quick fix" thinking abounds. In any direction you look there is the expectation of needs being met instantly. The information highway zooms whatever we need to know right in through our retinas, and pizza gets to our houses faster than the police. Micromedical techniques have surgeons re-attaching severed extremities like gods, and the removal of your gall bladder is outpatient surgery. We eat "fast food" in our cars and get impatient at home because the microwave takes so long. We can have an entire lawn put in before dark.

Since psychiatric wonder drugs treat our depression and anxiety, why shouldn't we expect religious professionals to give us "while-you-wait" healing and saving? We do. Bestselling religious books are packaged with extravagant promises, but inside they are thin as gruel. The way to grow a mega-church is to make the whole truth of God in Christ reducible to a gospel of simple answers and quick fixes.

The fix is in, but it is not quick. This is to say that forces of healing are at work in us and all around us, but they cannot be commanded or controlled. Dr. Rachel Naomi Remen, who specializes in the care of persons with life-threatening illnesses, says, "It's not what we do that makes a difference, but what we allow to happen. There is a natural process that moves towards wholeness in me and in every human being."[2] The providence of God has energized creation with powers that aim at wholeness, with processes of growth, renewal, and health. A process requires patience and trust.

When I prune my pyracantha, we generally exchange cuts. The scratches on my arms would devastate me if I thought they would never heal, and they would disappoint me if I expected them to heal instantly. It takes time, but the pyracantha and I both recover and live to fight another day. Sometimes the healing process needs nothing more from me than patience and trust.

In this regard our visible wounds are not appreciably different from our invisible ones. Grief behaves like the deep wound it is. It may become infected and need special treatment. It will probably leave a scar. However that may be, it is subject to a healing process that can be trusted.

See Life as a Gift

John Claypool, mentor and friend, has given me the best wisdom I have on grief. In a poignant, helpful book he wrote following his daughter's death, he allows us to listen in on his struggle. He found only one way down from, as he put it, "the Mountain of Loss." It was the way of seeing life as gift.

> At least it makes things bearable when I remember that Laura Lue was a gift, pure and simple, something I neither earned

nor deserved nor had a right to. . . . then I am better able to try and thank God that I was ever given her in the first place.[3]

The process that brings healing to our grief and guilt feelings will make sharp turns through many emotions, from anxiety to resignation to anger. There is no straight course through a wilderness. But gradually the most healing of all human perspectives will struggle to emerge. It is gratitude.

Creaturely praise is in our nature as it is in the songbird. We can choose the growing option of seeing all of life as a gift and seeing that the only proper response to a gift is gratitude.

There is a Camelot in my past. At least, it has seemed so these years since. I should more carefully factor in the human facility for over-remembering, but some days I see over my shoulder a time and a place of great happiness. I deeply regret the role I played in losing my residence there. A decade ago the guilt and grief were all-consuming. Now I, a scarred and wiser pilgrim, have found that life remains a journey, that the journey has very far horizons, and that the land of promise can be reached from anywhere.

When our past is seen less as a loss and more as a gift, we can cover it with a benediction of thanksgiving. "For all that has been, 'Thanks'; to all that will be, 'Yes!' "[4]

Notes

[1]Teilhard de Chardin, *Oeuvres*, Vol. 10 (Paris, 1969) 135-36.

[2]Quoted by Bill Moyers, *Healing of the Mind* (New York: Doubleday, 1993) 346.

[3]John Claypool, *Tracks of a Fellow Struggler* (Waco TX: Word, 1974) 82.

[4]Dag Hammarskjold, *Markings*, trans. Leif Sjoberg and W. H. Auden (New York: Alfred A. Knopf, 1964) 89.

4

Surviving Exile

Will you sit still for a Bible story? This story is important for people who have failed because it is about exile. Failure is always followed by feelings of exile, actual exile, or both. The story is also valuable because it involves both power failure and moral failure, as many serious failures do.

In the international politics of the time, the balance of world power had shifted to Babylonia, the Chaldean empire. Babylon had conquered both of the other superpowers, Assyria and Egypt. Inevitably, Nebuchadnezzar marched into Palestine, and it didn't take him long to capture the little nation of Judah. Some of the people were allowed to remain in and around Jerusalem, but among the many carried to Babylon were the king, the royal family, and most of the nation's intelligentsia. The Holy City never fully recovered from the deportation of 597 and the Babylonian exile.

Ever since this long-ago kidnapping of the Jews, Babylon has been stuck in their memory, epitomizing everything evil and godless. Centuries later another exile, on the island of Patmos, writing what would become the last book of the Bible, ascribed to the monstrous Roman empire the most terrible name he could think of. John called Rome "Babylon."

For a generation, back there in the sixth century B.C., Babylon became the Jews' home. Actually, they were treated relatively well, certainly better than they had fared in Egypt years before. But it was not home.

Has your soul ever sung the lament of homesickness? One of the most disturbed college students I ever saw, it turned out, was suffering from homesickness.

In Babylon, streams or canals connected the land between the great Tigris and Euphrates rivers. By these little rivers the exiled, alien people sat, talked, thought of home, and wept. "By the rivers of Babylon—there we sat down, and there we wept when we remembered Zion" (Ps 137:1).

To make matters worse, their captors goaded these uprooted people to sing some of the songs of their homeland. Cruel amusement. For the Jews, there were no songs of Zion (Jerusalem) that were not the Lord's songs. To sing these songs in a foreign land was a desecration, and to sing them as entertainment for heathens was unthinkable. "How," they cried, "could we sing the Lord's song in a foreign land?" (Ps 137:4). And they hung their lyres in the willow trees.

The penalty for failure is exile. The people of Judah were guilty of moral failure, as Jeremiah the prophet tried to make clear to them. They broke the covenant with God, which led, as it still does, to the breaking of other covenants. Then there were ill-advised political strategies, which resulted in power failure such as a lone mouse might experience in an alley full of cats. What made the Babylonian exile especially sorrowful was the excruciating knowledge that they had brought it on themselves.

Failure means we have to go. We can't stay. Things cannot remain as they were. The world is not built to absorb our failures and leave nothing unchanged. Isaac Newton's third law of physics, "For every action there is an equal and opposite reaction," is not without its personal and moral corollaries. Human actions have consequences. Life is moral to the core.

The grim possibilities of injustices, inequities, and inhumanity are necessary to a moral environment. They are moral consequences of human actions and systems that are immoral. Moral does not mean that I shoot a gun at someone and the bullet hits me. Such simple justice and instant retribution appeal to us. We think God should have created such a world. It would be a mechanical world, however, not a moral one. Moral means that the world of others is affected by my actions, for better or for worse, and I bear the responsibility. Moral means that the universe is a web of connectedness in which no acts are inconsequential, and the web extends both into my inner world and my outer world. Moral failure sends vibrations both directions, and neither world is ever exactly the same again.

Many people question how, in a moral world, six million innocent people could die in concentration camps. They miss the point. Only in a moral universe would it be possible, or matter. Life in general did not exterminate six million Jews; Hitler did. The shrieking echoes of cosmic offense at such a holocaust bear terrible witness to a moral framework in which such an act can happen but cannot be tolerated. Life is moral to the core.

Therefore, exile. Banishment is the punishment for failure, even if it is only banishment from our claims on innocence. The land of Nod, east of Eden, Babylonia of the Chaldeans—these are not remote in either time or space. We are there. We all know banishment from somewhere. We all live in exile from something.

During the last Holy Week of his life, Carlyle Marney said to the congregation I was serving that we all have to live in the wreckage of something that mattered but did not last. He said that during his Charlotte, North Carolina, years he kept several psychiatrists busy helping women in their twenties and thirties deal with the loss of their little girl images of themselves as wives and mothers.

Who is not exiled from a dream, an expectation, an intention? How will you survive your exile—if you do? How do we crash without burning? How do we endure the radical dislocation from cherished securities that failure can mean? The Babylonian exiles can help us.

Remembering Who We Are

By the rivers of Babylon the forlorn Jews surely wept, but their tears nourished and helped preserve the memory of who they were. "If I forget you, O Jerusalem, let my right hand wither! Let my tongue cling to the roof of my mouth, if I do not remember you, if I do not set Jerusalem above my highest joy" (Ps 137:5-6).

The people of Israel always found their identity in their history, their story. Who were they? They were the children of Abraham, Isaac, and Jacob. They were the slaves God had delivered from bondage. They were the ones to whom God had given the Law and the Land. When they strayed from their calling, their spiritual leaders stirred up the memory of who they were. Their faith and their identity were inseparable.

Who are we? Not knowing is being lost indeed. The most complete exile is not knowing who we are.

Who are we? I can only share my conviction, and it will either ring true or not. According to the biblical tradition, our fundamental identity is grounded in our source. We are the children of God. I am a child of God. I am not a little God, a smaller version of the original, but a creation of God. Something of my creator is in me. I am only I in relation to God's thou. My self, both conscious and unconscious, is a reflection of God's own selfhood.

More than I am a child of my parents, more than I am a citizen of any time or place, more than the sum total of my physical and psychological data, I possess a transcendent identity. This is no mystical, New Age, or esoteric suggestion. It is the conviction that no merely human categories completely define or exhaust my reality. It is a faith claim that my fullest identity is known only in relationship to God.

An experience of failure can ravage my sense of who I am. Whatever version of exile becomes my own particular sentence, it cuts me off from at least some of the relationships that have supported my understanding of myself. If too many planks in my sense of who I am are removed, I will fall into self-destructiveness. Suicide may involve a sudden and violent turning on oneself, or it may be subtle and progressive, a gradual detachment from my moorings.

In the 1950s, an African-American mother watched her son prepare to leave home because he was more a man than a boy, and a scholarship was waiting. She had cleaned houses to help give him what she never had. Now it was going to be his. However, it meant he was entering a strange world about which she knew little. She gave him all the motherly admonitions. Finally she said, "And, boy, don't you forget who you is."

We survive the foreign land to which failure consigns us, in large part, by remembering who we are. Our truest identity is not in geography; it is in our origin and our destiny.

Keeping Hope Alive

It was not only memory that kept those ancient Jews alive in Babylon. They survived by kindling a hope. They clung to the belief that the one in whom their memories were grounded would get them home again. They would not grant to their present reality the final word. They would see Jerusalem again! Once more they would sing the songs of Zion in the temple of the Lord!

The exiles' memory was the root system of a flowering hope. They were not mere nostalgics with rear vision only, living solely for the past. Memory, safeguarded in precious traditions, fueled the undying flame of anticipation. This deep memory spawned in them a great hope.

As memory is the gift of life from behind us, hope is the dynamic pull of life from before us. Ask the hospice nurse how much life there is after hope dies. Our endurance is literally, utterly dependent on keeping hope alive, and the strength of our hope will be the strength of our living.

Hoping in God is believing that all things that have a loving source also have a loving destiny. It is knowing that, as we have already experienced futures we could not have predicted, we still move toward futures beyond imagining. Just as our basic identity lies in our past and our origins, our completed identity waits in an unrealized future. The full story of who we are is in who we are becoming.

At the end of a child's sixth birthday, when she had been put to bed, her parents talked quietly as they cleaned up after the party. She smiled. "You know, you had such a good time today. But, I wondered something. Why did I see a little tear in your eye when she made her wish and blew out her candles? Were you thinking about when she was a little baby?" "No," he said with his own smile. "I was thinking about when she is going to be a woman."

"Beloved, we are God's children now; what we will be has not yet been revealed" (1 John 3:2).

Who Knew?

It is difficult to remember the worst of the feelings of first coming here, now over a decade ago. The facts are easier to recall and the glowing reports you gave others of your new situation. The dark, desperate aspects of those first experiences, however, slip away almost as soon as you grasp them. You would not have believed then that those rough, dry days would someday become such slippery memories.

The eyes of depression see nothing in its third dimension. There is no depth to anything or anyone, only a suffocating flatness. Our place of exile could be a Caribbean island five-star resort, and it would be to us as bleak as a Siberian winter.

This was an empty world, all form, no content, remote from meaning. You felt unknown and anonymous. Your surroundings seemed transient. You hoped they were. Other people held no interest for you. You wanted to be alone. When you were alone, you wanted someone there. You were acutely aware that out beyond your sensory limits, in an insulated channel of reality, your former world moved on without you, without requiring you. That knowledge accentuated the barrenness of your new home.

The lives, with imprisonment permanent and terminal, must make peace with the crumb of life that remains to keep from going mad. You found the courage to go on, with all things diminished. You gave up hope for happiness and settled for existence.

People from your family and your past would ask, in every communication, how you were. "Fine, really good, everything is going well." It was the least you could do after the grief you had caused them. Whether they believed it or not, maybe they would admire your grit.

One night, some years later, on the roof of your house where you and others are watching a fireworks display, you are surprised to realize that you are on the inside of yourself. You are not observing yourself, not monitoring your life from behind it. You look at the people you love, on the roof and in the yard. You look across your yard at the building where you work. You look up into a clear night. Everything is in 3-D. For the first time in years, and to your own amazement, you do not want to be anywhere but where you are.

The next time someone asks how you are doing, you don't answer as quickly. You say it slowly, this confession. "If you had told me when I came here that I would ever be as happy as I am now, I would have called you a liar."

Who knew?

Rethinking the World

The greatest discovery in our generation is that human beings, by changing the inner attitudes of their minds, can change the outer aspects of their lives.

—William James
The Principles of Psychology

5

The Environment of Failure

Comedian Flip Wilson and evangelist Jimmy Swaggart to the contrary notwithstanding, "the devil made me do it" is not an unacceptable excuse for moral failure. When Swaggart was caught in a New Orleans with a prostitute, he offered the following explanation. His evangelistic enterprises were so successful that the devil was being defeated and hurled back into darkness. The devil, therefore, launched a counterattack, lured Swaggart into a trap, and dealt a mortal blow to his soul-winning ministries.[1]

Whatever your doctrine of the devil, it is important that it not credit evil with the power to override human freedom. This would nullify any responsibility on my part, and my wrongdoing would not be a moral failure but only a power failure. Evil influences my actions only with my permission. A moral failure always results from a free decision.

Still, myriad and invisible influences lie behind any moral failure and are active in building the road to the critical decision. These influences will be as varied and as individual as we and our decisions are. When someone pulls a trigger, God only knows all the factors that contributed to that action.

Some influences are more general. They are as much a part of our environment as the air we breathe and may be inhaled just as unconsciously. These are the attitudes, perspectives, and values that are present in our families, our communities, and the larger culture. Our assimiliation of these influences may become the first steps toward failure.

The Myth of Self-Sufficiency

The myth of self-sufficiency is grounded in the idea that one can and should manage all personal conflicts and needs out of one's own strength. Help will be needed, of course, for broken bones, dented fenders, ping pong, and reproduction, but one should run one's department of the interior on one's own. A lot of pioneer stoicism, rugged individualism, and hardness of head have been bred into the average American.

Despite the strong images we present to each other, if you reach deep enough into any person you will find hurt. We all have inner wounds, whether we have acknowledged them or not. A wound needs tending. It is the nature of wounds to either heal or get worse. A wound that is not properly treated can worsen until it has poisoned and destroyed the whole organism. Some wounds we can treat ourselves, but not all. If we try to tend all our inner wounds out of our sense of self-sufficiency, we will eventually experience power failure, moral failure, or both.

The myth of self-sufficiency, any way you slice it, is a God complex. Carl Jung claimed that neuroses are failed attempts at self-healing. Where our deepest and truest needs are concerned, we cannot make it alone. You may be pretty impressive, but you are not God. We all need some other, a priestly friend, someone to whom we can tell anything and to whom we will not lie. We cannot heal ourselves of all that ails us. The myth of self-sufficiency can carry us far beyond our power limits.

It facilitates moral failure, too. If I handle all of my pain out of my self-sufficiency, I may substitute relief for healing. They are not the same. The alcoholic finds relief in another drink, but not healing. The need for healing in combination with a sense of self-sufficiency compounds the risk of moral failure.

You are in relational pain. You are in the grip of a deep and complex longing. You cannot, or do not, talk about it, either with your spouse or with anyone else. You are both too proud and too afraid. Then, mysteriously, someone is there, someone who soothes the pain. What exquisite relief! The gloom in you is lifted, not just for a few days, but for months, maybe years. You have never felt so complete, so confident, so alive. But, as emotionally and even spiritually gratifying as the relationship is, it is relief and not healing. In fact, it is relief at the expense of healing and results only in deepening and multiplying the pain.

The Myth of Success

Ironically, the worship of success breeds failure. This, of course, is contrary to the accepted dogma. No matter. We would flatly deny that we worship at this shrine anyway. The worship of success, like any respectable idolatry, involves some self-deception and the shutting of at least one eye. Our actual objects of worship are not usually those named in our official creeds. The task of a lifetime, even for the most sincere, can be the matching of one's life to one's creed. Lip service is more convenient.

Throughout our culture nothing is credited with as much actual value as success. We are culturally programmed to feel that it doesn't matter so much what we do as long as we are successful at it.

It isn't just success. Success is a word that can be twisted to mean anything we deem good. The measure of all things for us tends to be success by quantitative standards. Bigger is better, and it's the Super Bowl or bust.

We find ingenious ways to justify our worship, even to ourselves. We put such a shine on it that we never think to question it. We're so smart, we can fool ourselves. For years I heard my home denomination's classic rationalization for being preoccupied with numerical growth and expansionistic ambitions. It was evangelism. Rescue theology is difficult to argue if you buy its premise. Then, if you are dedicated enough in trying to get all the sheep into the safety of the fold, who can criticize you if you inadvertently become the largest sheepholder in the county?

Pastors are always asked how large their churches are. When I was the pastor of a 3,000-member church, I would get star treatment for just answering the question honestly. "Oh, you're a successful pastor!" Our most telling cultural tragedy may be the triumph of quantitative values in the very institutions that had their origins in a commitment to quality of life.

I heard the late George Buttrick say near the end of his life how bored he got with success stories. What this country needed, he said, was a few "noble failures."

Where success is the ultimate good, failure is the supreme evil. Suicide statistics say something about how many of us would literally rather die than fail. Therefore, our striving may become so urgent that certain moral boundaries are crossed without hesitation, so certain are we that the end justifies the means. Also, such striving often becomes so all-consuming that vast regions of our lives go unattended, until the ecological balance is tipped and a desert appears. So, what is the bottom line on reaching the top and losing your soul?

The Myth of Happiness

The cultural myth of happiness rests on two assumptions: (1) Happiness is a right. (2) Happiness is circumstantial.

In a narcissistic environment, where one's self is the supreme reality, it is unquestioned that the pursuit of happiness will be the basic human quest, and should be. If you ask, "What's wrong with that?" you help make my point. It is unthinkable to us that anyone this side of a Puritan pulpit would inveigh against happiness.

To be sure, being happy beats being sad. I am serious in my desire for happiness, especially for the people I love most, but also for myself. The tragic error, however, is in thinking that happiness is an inalienable right, and that, therefore, its pursuit is meritorious.

One characteristic of a "land of liberty" is the freedom or right of all citizens to pursue their own happiness, but that does not make possessing it an individual right or pursuing it a worthy goal. Both ideas are mistaken, and the pursuit of happiness is ultimately self-defeating.

Most things are acquired by going after them directly. When our earliest primogenitors saw something that stirred a basic appetite, they picked up a club and went straight after it. It is a course of action based on one of the few geometric principles I understand: The shortest distance between two points is a straight line. As infants we gradually learned how to focus on and then reach for objects in the small world around us. We've been reaching for things ever since. It is one of our fundamental moves. It is an obvious simplicity that we get what we want by going directly after it.

Clearly, however, there are some things we do not acquire by going after them. There are some things that come to us when we have gone after something else. Happiness is supreme among these. Happiness is a byproduct. It is the byproduct of responsible living and relating. It is not a suitable goal, but the serendipitous gift of proper goal seeking. When we pursue happiness for itself, we are least likely to find it. It must almost be forgotten to be found.

The point is, some of the most unfortunate decisions we make arise out of the unexamined conviction that happiness is both our right and a worthy goal. "I'm unhappy" is used to justify everything.

The second misguided assumption in this cultural myth is that happiness is circumstantial. In other words, happiness is the product of the right set of external circumstances. If asked what it would take to make us happy, most of us would answer in terms of some change in our circumstances. We have adopted the wisdom of commercial real estate: It's location, location, location. Many of us are certain that we are in the wrong one.

In the 1800s, when wagon trains followed the Oregon Trail to the promised land of the American West, more persons wanted to go than went. One fellow who lived in Missouri, where the famous route began, was always talking about

Oregon. He spoke with all the people he could who were making the trek and obviously fantasized about going himself. One day a friend who was tired of hearing it said, "Why are you always carrying on about Oregon? What makes you think Oregon is so wonderful? Have you ever been there?" "No," the man replied, "but I've been here."

The evidence is strong, however, that external circumstances cannot guarantee either happiness or unhappiness. Between the extremes of unrelieved suffering and transcendent joy, the influence of circumstances seems fairly inconsistent. One couple can marry and spend their lives in palatial luxury and be perpetually miserable, while another couple can go from the altar to a lifetime of bliss in a double-wide.

My friend Clyde Fant has a proverb: "Nothing is as good as it looks when you are not there." When the Babylonian captivity of the Jews finally ended in 539 B.C., and Cyrus the Great allowed the exiles to return to Judah and beautiful Jerusalem, two strange things happened. First, those who returned, who had wept bitter tears at the memory of Zion, found in the ruins of their homeland neither what they remembered nor what they had hoped for. Second, some of those displaced Jews did not return at all, because after half a century, the despised place of exile had become a home they did not wish to leave.

Happiness is not in location, except maybe for a short vacation. Happiness is in relationships, in being rightly related to yourself, to other people, and to God. Here is one of those things we know, but cannot believe, which is harder. Happiness is not circumstantial but relational.

An Anti-Environmental Movement

Truth has little respect for the principle of majority rule and has historically traveled with a minority. In the Bible it is the principle of the remnant, usually with a scenario something like this. The covenant is broken. God's people have been unfaithful. The Almighty is in such indignation that it looks like curtains on the human drama. But when the anguish of judgment is over and the dust settles, there is always a little band of the surviving faithful moving out into the future singing, "Glory, hallelujah!" It is God's truth marching on.

You can find it everywhere, this anti-environmental movement, this crosscurrent, this minority report. Always, on the darkest night, one tiny far-off star that will not let the light die. Always, in a walled-in world of bondage, a way out, an exodus, the unlikely persistence of God's truth.

The revolutionary remnant is seldom a predictable group, certainly not always from the religious establishment. God has never been above using outsiders, and our poets and artists have often been our prophets. Today, in fact, we see a terrible trend, one recurrent in history, of the officially religious increasingly facing in the same direction as everyone else, going with the prevailing winds. Much preaching reinforces the cultural myths of self-sufficiency, success, and happiness, and then promises that Jesus is the means to those ends. Institutional religion has always capitulated to its cultural environment, but the genuinely prophetic voices have consistently been spiritual anti-environmentalists.

All human environments, even the best, have deceptive enticements that set us up for failure. The Genesis story of the Fall tells us this. All life is lived to the east of Eden. All geographical points lie outside the garden. No physical place is worthy of our permanent citizenship, or even our full weight. One goal of growth in faith is to be *in* the world but not *of* the world. This mature perspective is not escapist (we remain *in* the world), and it is not conformist (we are not *of* the world). Therefore, it has the possibility both of transcending and of transforming the environment of failure.

Note

[1]John Shelby Spong, *Rescuing the Bible from Fundamentalism* (San Francisco: HarperSanFrancisco, 1992) 3.

6

"The Vale of Soul Making"

Consider the word "valley." How many phrases can you think of that have the word valley in them? Vale, which is a synonym, is acceptable.

"How green was my valley!" Good. "From the valley of the Jolly, ho, ho, ho, Green Giant." Barely acceptable. "The lily of the valley." "The valley of the shadow of death." "Peace in the valley." " This vale of tears." Ezekiel's "valley of dry bones." Bunyan's "valley of humiliation." Susann's "valley of the dolls." Tennyson's "valley of death," into which rode the six hundred. The prophet Joel's "valley of decision." Gray's "cool sequestered vale of life." Coleridge's "scanty vale of human life." Excellent.

You have demonstrated what a common and useful metaphor the valley has been found to be. Often it has represented the most comprehensive realities: life, the world.

Hold that thought.

Less than three years after receiving the Nobel Prize in Literature, while returning to Paris from the south of France, on January 4, 1960, Albert Camus was killed in an automobile crash. Brilliant, sensitive, he was a true philosopher in that he knew this: "Judging whether life is or is not worth living amounts to answering the fundamental question of philosophy."[1]

Though fundamental, this is a question some people never ask, the many who never step back far enough from the canvas to see the picture whole. Yet, the question of life's meaning precedes and underlies all other concerns. Those who do not ask the question are still under its ubiquitous influence. Even when the meaningfulness of life is an unexamined assumption, as it is in all our lighter and brighter moments, we reveal in a thousand ways that our lives are anchored in a need for meaning. We cannot tolerate an utterly chaotic environment (although to adults, adolescents seem to), and whatever order we impose, even if it makes sense only to us, reflects this human essential. We require structures of meaning in the simplest forms of communication and can be driven mad by unremitting incoherence. As distinguished from creatures of instinct, we humans are creatures of meaning. And the deeper our sense of meaning, the riper and fuller our humanity.

This is not an intellectual matter, as some might suppose, but a spiritual one. Brilliant Martin Buber, in his classic *I and Thou*, claims that God and the search for meaning are bound up with each other. "Meeting with God does not come to man in order that he may concern himself with God, but in order that he may confirm that there is meaning in the world."[2]

Failure sometimes becomes a person's first serious occasion for questioning the meaning of life. When you are standing in the rubble of a collapsed world, trying to decide if the pieces are even worth picking up, you may find yourself asking some pretty heavy questions. Even a simple "why me?" tossed flippantly skyward when we have stumped a toe implies most aspects of our struggle for meaning.

When the fundamental question is asked, there are endlessly varied answers. To record them all, much less discuss them, would take volumes. However, to satisfy me, at least, all must:

- acknowledge the human need for meaning
- ask the question of God's existence and nature
- take into account the reality of evil and suffering

Those who attempt religious interpretations of the meaning of life face a classic dilemma. If God is both all-powerful and all-loving, how do you explain the undeniable presence and persistence of evil in the world? It must be that God is either not all-powerful or not all-loving. Why does God not destroy evil and eradicate suffering? Is it that God *would* if God *could* (all-loving but not all-powerful)? Or is it that God *could* if God *would* (all-powerful but not all-loving)? Either option is devastating to the concept of God and gives the victory to evil.

Some consider John Keats the most gifted poet of the English Romantic period. His work is made more impressive with the knowledge that he died at age twenty-five. In a letter to his brother and sister, George and Georgiana, on April 21, 1819, John Keats wrote, "Call the world if you please 'the vale of soul making.' Then you will find out the use of the world."[3]

What kind of valley is it that all mortals traverse? Is it an accidental valley, the result of blind processes of nature, or left by a God who created it and then abandoned it? Is it a happy valley, all peace and beauty, where we anticipate only good things from a beneficent and omnipresent God? Is it a dark valley, a descent only, with horizons disappearing in the inevitable process of our disintegration and decay? Is it the valley of Ecclesiastes, a world of vanities where the best we can do is eat, drink, look good, and marry well?

Or is it a valley whose purpose is the making of souls, in which what begin as infantile, almost cellular images of God are provided an environment that is conducive to nothing so much as their growth into the fullness of the Creator's intention? Think what represents the most divine possibility in the realm of our human potential. Not success by human standards. That offers brief satisfaction at best. Not longevity or prosperity or good health, all fine commodities, but pointless as ends in themselves. Nothing we buy or sell in the markets of this world, or seek. The most divine possibility of our created humanity is growing up into oneness with God. Could my response to life ever be such that my own identity becomes lost, or fulfilled, in God's?

The valley is in some sense all the things we and others have said. It is primarily, I think, the vale of soul-making, a realm where nothing is useless to God's purpose, no flaw, no pain, no loss, and no failure we can name or imagine.

Notes

[1] Albert Camus, *The Myth of Sisyphus and Other Essays*, trans. Justin O'Brien (New York: Alfred A. Knopf, 1955) 3.

[2] Martin Buber, *I and Thou* (New York: Scribner's, 1955) 115.

3John Keats, *Selected Poems and Letters*, ed. Douglas Bain (Boston: Houghton Mifflin, 1959) 288.

7

What Cannot Be Shaken

Hear my defense of Murphy's Law, which reads in its official form: "If anything can go wrong, it will."[1] Perhaps you think it doesn't need defending since your own life is daily verification of it.

Murphology is lighthearted cynicism. The original law has been elaborated in endless corollaries. Some of us have developed our own. Murphology addresses the pessimistic streak in us and enables us to laugh at it.

I want to suggest that Murphy's Law is based on serious reality and has theological significance. I am not a murphological fundamentalist, so I'm not advocating a literal interpretation of the law. Obviously, *everything* that can go wrong, meaning every instance of that possibility, does not happen. I once had an acute appendicitis attack while in the pulpit and passed out. But only once. Every time I go into a pulpit it does not happen, and most other preachers do not have appendicitis attacks while in the pulpit. Therefore, my modification of Murphy's Law is: "If anything can go wrong, it will . . . at least once."

I admit this is more of a theory than a law. There are loopholes and exceptions to most laws anyway, except what has been called "the law of love." But I theorize with relative confidence that, with regard to this mortal and material world, every negative possibility we can think of has happened or will happen somewhere, sometime.

Now if you start thinking of negative impossibilities, you are not playing fair. Steve Martin once did a parody on the song "It's Impossible," and he had lines in it such as, "It's impossible to stick a piano up your nose, it's just impossible." That kind of thinking misses my point. I am referring to negative possibilities in this real world of matter, space, and time.

This is important to me, even if I am wrong, as a way of demonstrating how susceptible the world all about us is to failure. Failure is not limited to the human species. The alarm clock fails to alarm. The percolator fails to perc. The toaster fails to toast. The car breaks down on the way to work. The pay phone is dead. No taxis appear. Bus drivers are on strike. Your shoes start hurting your feet after about a block. You get to work, and your computer goes berserk during sermon preparation. On Sunday, your appendix goes berserk mid-sermon delivery. The doctor's name is Murphy.

This is somehow theological? Yes, it is seriously theological. It affirms the Godness of God.

During one of the shakiest periods of my faith journey I read Paul Tillich's sermon, "The Shaking of the Foundations." It would have been frightening and threatening to me at most previous times, but apparently this was the fullness of time, and it was an epiphany. It opened a door at the end of a corridor. It offered me an expansive God for my expanding world.

It confirmed my theological version of Murphy's Law: "Whatever can be shaken, will be shaken." That's what Tillich was saying, I think. He just didn't have Murphy's Law.

Throughout biblical history idolatry was a subject of both horror and fascination. Idolatry was the most sorrowful of possibilities to a sovereign God and to God's prophets, yet it was a unending temptation to God's people. "Thou shalt have no other gods before me," demands a God whom the Bible calls "jealous"—not jealous in our petty, self-centered sense, but jealous in not wanting us to choose any way but the way of life.

If God is to be clearly perceived as God, all else will need to be seen as not-God. The problem with idolatry is that it is unreal. It has no foundation; therefore, it has no future. I believe that one of the functions of the historical process is to separate the wheat from the chaff, to sift what is not-God from the one true God, to expose the false and reveal the true. What we may not see as it is unfolding will ultimately be realized as the clarification of all things. "For now we see in a mirror, dimly, but then we will see face to face" (1 Cor 13:12a).

This bit of theological reflection may shed positive and redemptive light on human failure. If my experiences of failure do not defeat me, they may help me see more clearly what does not fail. If human history involves the shaking of what can be shaken, then it can also be the source of knowing what cannot be shaken.

Tillich speaks of the Eternal as being "the foundation on which all foundations are laid," and says, "this foundation cannot be shaken." He contends that "there is something immovable, unchangeable, unshakeable, eternal, which becomes manifest in our passing and in the crumbling of our world." He says that "on the boundaries of the finite the infinite becomes visible."[2]

Tillich's words speak to me. I believe this quite fervently on my good days, when the sun is shining and my work seems worthwhile and my relationships are working out. But when I am in the darkness and dizziness that follow failure, I may doubt it.

One way or another we are affected by our failures. Some times failure affects us so drastically as to be life-threatening. Precipitous to some suicides is the feeling that nothing is infallible, that nothing can be trusted. My failure may shake the foundations of my life so violently that I question whether anything holds.

The experience of failure can push faith beyond its limits. I may believe with all my heart in the unshakeable One of whom Tillich and the prophets of every age have spoken. But failure can throw all my systems into a new gear, and the things I believe most earnestly may become suspect.

In every crisis I have experienced, the counsel has come from someone, usually more than one, to have faith. "Keep the faith," I am told, and have told others. It's good advice. But what do I do when faith vanishes, even when I have done the best I can to keep it?

I do not speak for everyone at this point, but, while the One in whom I have faith may be unshakeable, the beams that buttress my personal faith are shakeable. How much easier life would be with an unshakeable faith. A part of me has always envied those who never need to ask the boundary questions. What a carefree way to live. It is not a gift I have been given, however, and I have come to the conclusion that, for me, faith must be wide-eyed and uncompromising if it is to bear the weight of my life.

My faith is sometimes threatened because my emotions have been shaken. I become so emotionally distraught that I have no feelings, no conscious sense of the presence of God. My emotions are so shakeable that I cannot always trust them in a crisis.

My reasoning faculties are shakeable, too, and when I am depressed or in a crisis, my thought processes become irrational and even nihilistic. I may find that the rational foundation of my confidence in God is gone.

My faith is not invulnerable. Knock the props of emotion and reason out from under it, and my faith will probably fall.

Still, there is that which cannot be shaken. There is One who, beyond the collapse of everything, remains. My world of experience may be feeble and ultimately fallible, but that does not affect the unshakeableness of the Unshakeable.

Faith, as I have known it, may be one of the casualties of failure. My unfortunate choices or fatal decisions may force me beyond the boundaries of my belief system, beyond the spiritual resources of my daily life. So, what do we do when even faith is gone?

We hang on. What do we have to lose? We wait for the return of faith. Probably our faith was too small anyway.

Hanging on in the dark and slippery miasma that follows failure will lead, I am confident, to the unexpected sighting of a distant light and the almost shocking feeling in the feet of solid ground.

Considerably more serious than the pleasant cynicism of Murphy's Law is the strange possibility that every instance of human failure is a negative verification of the sovereignty of God. What can be shaken will be shaken. What cannot be shaken will be revealed.

Notes

[1]Arthur Bloch, *Murphy's Law and Other Reasons Why Things Go Wrong!* (Los Angeles: Price/Stern/Sloan, 1979) 11.

[2]Paul Tillich, *The Shaking of the Foundations* (New York: Charles Scribner's Sons, 1948) 9.

8

The Size and Shape of Truth

What do we do when our world is not large enough to absorb or even contain our failure?

As a pastor I have known several families in which one family member accused another family member of involving or attempting to involve them in some kind of inappropriate sexual activity. These have all been enormously traumatic situations, with the difficulty of knowing whom to believe creating among family members deep ruts of suspicion and mistrust that might never be healed.

In one of these situations, the accused person, an adult male, was fairly quickly absolved to the satisfaction of his entire family of the claims made by a preteen female. One day in the aftermath of that storm he told me that he had thought about what it would be like to be guilty of those accusations. He said, "I decided there was nowhere I could go that would be far enough to get away from that."

The world sometimes seems too small to contain our transgressions. Therefore, because we cannot reverse time and erase our failures, we must look for a larger world.

The Size of Truth

Perhaps one reason we cannot find the edges or boundaries of our universe is so there are no limits, except within us, on how large the world can be. It's not a scientific hypothesis, but think about it a moment. What if the only limit to the size of your world is the size of your imagination, or your perception, or your will? What if God has created a world that is endlessly adaptable to our changing and increasing capacities?

At different points in our lives we do, in fact, decide on the size of our world. Some experience may expose my world as too small. It was Sibelius, I think, who said of Marian Anderson that his roof was too low for such a voice. Growth results from our willing response to the necessity of raising our roofs. It sounds like fun, but it is usually painful and can be excruciating.

We also come to those times, say, when we are ill or growing old, when there is the need to reduce the size of our worlds. The human spirit is so tenacious that this, too, can be difficult, if not impossible, to accept. Generally, I find that either enlarging or decreasing the size of your world requires the help of others.

Failure often produces the sensation that the world has become very small, almost claustrophobic. Hopelessness may creep in with the realization that there is no undoing of what is done. We have made history. Even beyond whatever restitution is possible and whatever forgiveness can be found, we must find a larger world as the context of our failure.

How do you picture God? Whether you believe in God or not, there is probably some kind of image in your mind. When you were eight years old, you may have thought of God as a celestial Santa, or a cosmic policeman, or a kindly though boring grandfather. Maybe you still do, but your world has expanded since you were eight, even if your image of God has not.

J. B. Phillips wrote a little classic some years ago entitled *Your God Is Too Small.* It wasn't for eight-year-olds. It was for everybody. Whoever you are, and however you picture God, your concept of God is smaller than the reality. Phillips affirmed that God is always larger than, greater than, and far beyond even our best concepts and images.

Idolatry today often means not simply putting something godless in the place of God, though that is still done, but identifying God with one particular image or idea of God. Maybe it comes from when you were eight. It's amazing to me how otherwise intelligent and sophisticated people can go through life with childish concepts of God. Any time you identify God exclusively with one particular conception or image, you are not only doing a disservice to God but putting a ceiling on your life at a critical point. It becomes a subtle form of idolatry.

Suppose you have an uncle in Australia. You haven't seen him in twenty years, because Australia is a long way away. But you have a picture of him that was taken the last time you were together. It was when you visited Australia twenty years ago. That picture is in a visible place in your house, and you look at it often. That is your Uncle Harry in Australia. That is the way he looks. That is the color of his hair. That is the slightly odd way he dresses. The picture keeps you in touch with Uncle Harry.

Suppose, after so long a time, Uncle Harry visits America and comes to see you. One thing is certain. He will not be the person in that picture. Twenty years change the face, the color, the shape of almost everything, except perhaps, plastic.

When you see him, your private self may feel like shouting, "You're not my uncle! Uncle Harry has dark brown hair, not yellowish white hair. He is taller than you and has wider shoulders. He has no wrinkles in his face. Come, let me show you a picture of Uncle Harry, and then we'll find out who you are, you impostor!"

Get the point? Maybe you are thinking the analogy does not hold. Uncle Harry in Australia changes, to be sure. He is human and timebound. God does not change. But you do. Is that really you standing next to Uncle Harry in the venerated photograph? Funny, it hardly looks like you.

Never, not at any point in your life, no matter how much you change, do you even come close to encompassing the whole reality of God. Maybe you are working with a picture of God from some time in your past that was meaningful and adequate for that time, and freezing it into a frame, then living your life with the assumption that *that* is God, right over there. Or maybe you are working with some image of God that the people around you seem to accept, that a large part of your culture reinforces, and maybe you are assuming that the God business is settled, and you can move on to other things.

It is God in a box. God? Oh, yes. God is over there in that box. My saintly mother gave it to me when I was a child. Or, my high school Sunday School teacher gave it to me. Or, I got it at a Billy Graham crusade in 1975. Or, my favorite professor in college gave it to me. Whatever. It is God in a box. It is a framed picture of God.

What is the problem? It is the same problem we have with any idolatry. We forfeit the living God.

For several years the conviction has grown in me that the major dividing line in the world of faith is not between such traditional antagonists as Catholics and Protestants, or even liberals and conservatives, and it is certainly not between any of the mainline denominations, all of which have some of everything in their camps and don't know what to do about it. The great division, it seems to me, is between what I choose to call sectarian faith and world faith.

Sectarian faith is provincial. It works from a given, ready-made worldview. It knows where the edges and boundaries of the universe are. "Here is how the world is," says sectarian faith. "Accept it. Don't ask questions about it. Trust the authority of those who have been granted authority. When the experiences of your life or the realities of the world seem to contradict this worldview, those experiences and realities must be denied. The real test of faith is how faithful you can remain to this world view that has been given to you. Don't let outside influences cause you a moment of doubt."

This is sectarian faith, whatever its individual expressions. Do you see the size of its truth? Truth is both comprehensible and containable. The world is constricted. You can build a fence around it, like someone's back yard.

I can relate to this because I see now how sectarian my own religious background was. Southern Baptists in Texas might not have techically qualified as a sect when I was growing up, primarily because we were a majority. Sects were Jehovah's Witnesses, Mormons, Christian Scientists, and such. But I realize now that we were provincial, locked in to an unquestioned worldview, and exclusivistic.

We seriously wondered whether members of other Christian denominations were really Christians, and we *knew* the Catholics were not. We were God's people, the true recipients of God's truth, and we bore an evangelistic responsibility for the rest of the world. It was a worldview so narrow, a conception of God so small, that it did not carry me past my seventeenth year, though I clung to its wreckage for at least ten years more.

Such fundamentalism makes the reality of God small. It does this by saying, "The way we think of God is exactly the way God is." God is contained. The truth is, of course, that the living God is not small enough to be captured by or corraled in any system of thought or faith.

At Stetson University a few years ago I heard Ruth Tiffany Barnhouse, psychiatrist, Episcopal priest, and grandmother, use a helpful metaphor. She suggested that we imagine a large mobile made up of a thousand pieces of stained glass, all different colors. You've seen mobiles. You move one part, and the whole thing moves. Imagine that this mobile is hanging in a doorway so that it is affected by sunlight and wind from outside, as well as by inside influences. If you sat in a chair and looked at that mobile for the rest of your life, it would never from one moment to the next look exactly the same to you. The central identity of the mobile would remain the same, but it would never look exactly the same way twice. Then, she said, at the end of your life you might realize that, if you had sat in a different chair just a few feet over, you'd have had a slightly different experience.

It is a wonderful metaphor for the Bible. Who reads it, or sees its truth, in exactly the same way? The fact that we have the

Bible is no guarantee of anything, certainly not the nailing down of a final and unassailable worldview.

World faith resists giving supremacy to any provincial perspective, while valuing and learning from all of them as ways of seeing. World faith is willing to have its worldview changed. World faith believes that all truth is God's truth, and, therefore, that truth can be trusted and followed wherever it is found. World faith says, "Believe in God, not in a worldview. Believe that God is greater than all of our conceptions, and that discovering the reality of God is a never-ending pilgrimage. Honestly question all authority claims, and be suspicious of easy answers. Let the experiences of your life and the realities of the world interact with your beliefs, so that you may continue to grow. Believe that God is love, and that whatever contradicts love is not of God. Do not assume that you understand Jesus, but follow him and see where he takes you. Do not put either the Word of God of the Spirit of God in a straitjacket. Learn to live with mystery and a certain degree of uncertainty. Keep your heart and mind open, so that you will be free to follow whatever light you receive, as long as it is light."

The possibility of a such faith should be good news to all who have failed and think the world cannot contain their failure. Truth is the size of reality itself, and God is the source of all truth. We do not need either to be afraid of truth or to defend truth. We need to trust truth wherever we find it.

The Shape of Truth

Someone will say, "Well, then, if truth is so large, so vast, so all-encompassing, it doesn't matter what we believe, as long as we're open-minded and sincere." Someone will say, "There is truth, then, in all religions, and we're all on a track toward the same destination and the same God." Someone will ask, "If truth has this universal dimension, why not just believe a little bit of everything?"

To say that truth is the size of reality itself is not to say that everything in the world qualifies as truth. Even if there is truth in most religions, that does not mean that all religions are essentially the same or that they have equal value. A religion that teaches the value of all human life is superior to a religion that practices child sacrifice. A religion that upholds the ideal of peace is superior to a religion that advocates holy war.

I hear the Bible say that something of God's truth is available to everyone and is known by everyone. There is the claim in Acts 14:17 that among the nations of the earth God has not been left without a witness. The apostle Paul claims that something of God can be known by everyone through the world of nature and through the conscience. The prologue to John's Gospel has this wonderful verse: "The true light, which enlightens everyone was coming into the world" (John 1:9). The light that is found in Jesus is the light that enlightens every person. However, this universality of God's truth does not mean that God's truth is everywhere and in everything equally revealed. Also, the universal size of God's truth does not mean that God's truth has no specific shape.

Rural America has always had a lot of jokes about preachers and fried chicken. I will spare you my favorites. It was not just that preachers were fed a lot of fried chicken by their members, but that they had such a fondness and such capacities for it. Gluttony has never been a popular subject with the clergy. I, therefore, freely confess my own weakness for fried chicken. I confess it readily also because it is one of my lesser vices. My favorite piece of chicken is the wing. Give me the wings, and you can have the rest. You say, "But it's all chicken." I won't argue with that. It *is* all chicken. So, I say to you, "Here, have some feathers, or a beak, or some feet. It's all chicken." Like you, you see, there are many more parts of a chicken that I will not eat than I will eat.

All truth is God's truth, but all truth is not of equal importance. Some of God's universal truth is pretty mundane and pedestrian. I am convinced, however, that the essence, the core, the center of God's truth has a very specific shape.

My friend Glenn Hinson, professor of church history and spirituality, says that God has a center but no circumference. There is a heart out of which divine love and power flow, but there are no outer limits.

God's truth, which is universal in its size, has a very specific shape. What shape? As far back as we can see, cave drawings and stone artifacts have aimed at representing the Eternal. Today we can reproduce any particular shape with a vast variety of materials; yet, despite our spiritual urges, we have seldom gotten beyond the trinkets and symbols of our superficial culture.

What shape? I will give you my answer. We will look more closely at its implications later, but, if someone is needing to rethink the world, I offer this observation for consideration. I keep finding at reality's heart a cruciform.

Crosses are everywhere today. They are worn by the priests of our culture, such as rock stars and athletes, as much as by the ordained of the church. Today crosses are valued for their aesthetic appeal or for some private emotional connection, as if they had no past, no history. The cross has become a talisman, a malleable symbol that can represent anything.

The cross is historical, however, and specific in meaning. It was an ancient instrument of capital punishment, made famous primarily by the death of Jesus. For followers of Jesus, it represents the death of death, the offering of life. It is the new beginning, as we measure time. A.D. *Annos Domini*. It is also timeless newness for all who will embrace its meaning.

What meaning? The cross of Jesus is the supreme revelation of God as love and of love as self-giving. Sacrifice is not so much something offered to God as what God offers to us: self-sacrificing love.

My failure is not too large for God's world or too extreme to threaten God's truth. My failure is held, held by arms of infinite reach, extending from a heart of perfect love.

9

Learning to Pray

In a Holiday Inn north of Jacksonville, Florida, somewhere between what was and whatever will be, it is after midnight and you cannot pray. You have never felt so alone. A rented trailer is parked outside, its size a sad symbol of how little from your life has been preserved. You try to pray once more for the undoing of what had been done. You desperately want someone to rush in, as parents do with a child, and begin cleaning up the humiliating mess you have made. You want a miracle nullifying the laws of cause and effect, a reprieve from the bleak consequences that lie in every direction you look. You wish the phone to ring, although no one in the world knows where you are, and you are not sure who cares.

Your whispers of remorse and petitions for help do not penetrate even the popcorn surface of the dropped ceiling above you. Nor do your words rebound or create an echo, but vanish as soon as they are out of your mouth. Finally you pray only to sleep, your body both dead with fatigue and rigid with anxiety.

All of your life you have been told that, whatever happens, prayer is an unfailing resource. When there is nothing else to do, you can always pray. How many stories have you heard about answered prayer in the extremities of some motel room? But you cannot pray. You wonder if your failure has cost you even this, life's last resort.

The Meaning of Prayer

Mothers are often the first instructors in prayer. Praying has never been big as a masculine activity, so fathers are mainly busy teaching us how to live in such a way that we will never need to pray. The first prayer most of us learned was the famous "Now I lay me down to sleep," which turned out to be surprisingly morbid when we realized we were saying, "If I should die before I wake." You pray that prayer and then lie there in the dark finding all kinds of symptoms of your imminent death.

My mother was not teaching me so much *how* to pray as impressing on me the importance of praying. Learning how to pray may be the business of a lifetime, and that may not be long enough. In the meantime, one way or another, we eventually pray.

How we pray says everything about how we understand God. How we understand God in our culture is, for the most part, as the Great Meeter of our Needs. When I make myself the center of the universe, I tend to see everything else revolving around me, even God. Self-centeredness is serious. It forces everything else into an orbit. While I may have a theoretical belief that God is the center of all things and should be acknowledged as such, at the practical level I deceive myself. This human capacity for self-deception is both ancient, chronic, and impressive.

When do most people pray? Factor out the genuinely religious, the fashionably pious, and New Age spiritualists. When do most people pray? When they need something or want something, and usually the two are thought to be the same.

Be honest. When was the last time you prayed? You needed something, right? Maybe not a "thing." After all, you're not a materialist. But you had a need. You needed strength, or confidence, or wisdom. You needed to be calm, at peace about something. You needed forgiveness. Or maybe you just needed to know that you were loved. All good things. The point is, we pray when we need something. We use God like an ATM.

When we have failed, we have many needs. The failed pray a lot—or try to pray. The experience of failure not only drives us to prayer, but may become a catalyst in learning how to pray. The great preacher Harry Emerson Fosdick, first pastor of Riverside Church, New York City, had a nervous breakdown while he was preparing for the ministry. In his autobiography he says of his time of recovery, "I learned to pray, not because I had adequately argued out prayer's rationality, but because I desperately needed help from a Power greater than my own."[1]

What is prayer? Formulated words? Petitions? Confession? Intercession? All of these, but they are secondary categories. Prayer is not merely communication; it is interpersonal communication. Interpersonal communication happens between one self and another self. God is not some supernatural official before whom we appear, such as a judge or a school principal. God is personal, a person. God is a self, the Self in whom all selves are grounded. Martin Buber has taught us to think of God not as an "It," but as a "Thou." Interpersonal communication involves the possibility of intimacy. Can there be intimacy with God?

A Theology Lesson

One of the ways to follow Christian thought down through the centuries is to see it swinging or alternating between two poles concerning God. These two poles are the transcendence of God on the one hand, and the immanence of God on the other.

The transcendence of God has to do with God's otherness, holiness, and qualitative difference from everything else. The transcendent God is God the Beyond, God the Ground of all being, God the incomprehensible and unapproachable Mystery. This is the One of whom we sing, "Holy, Holy, Holy! Lord God Almighty!"

The immanence of God has to do with God's nearness and presence with us and in us. This is the One whom we have said is closer than breathing and nearer than our hands and feet.

Throughout history theologians and biblical scholars have tended to emphasize either the transcendence or the immanence of God. They usually did this in reaction to whatever was the mood of their time. For example, nineteenth-century liberal theologians emphasized the immanence of God so thoroughly that they almost made divinity an aspect of our humanity. God was understood to be with us so completely as to almost be dissolved in us. Humanity was capable of infinite possibilities and unlimited progress. Then, in the early part of the twentieth century, the Swiss theologian Karl Barth wrote a commentary on the Epistle to the Romans. It is said to have been like a bombshell dropped on the playground of the theologians. Barth had rediscovered in the Bible the radical transcendence of God, God as Wholly Other, God who is beyond all things, certainly beyond our reach. This emphasis ended up requiring some correctives, too, but this is one way Christian thought has developed.

Which is correct? Is God transcendent or immanent? Is God far beyond us or very near to us? It is a paradoxical truth, but we cannot do justice to the Bible if we exclude either God's transcendence or God's immanence. God is both.

The most popular brand of Christianity today is so focused on the immanence of God, on intimacy with God, as to be in danger of losing any sense whatsover of the transcendence of God. The stress is so much on God *with us* and *in us* that God's holy otherness is lost.

Whatever intimacy with God means, it does not mean a diminishing of God's Godness, a loss of the mystery that is essential to God. The Bible knows nothing about chumminess with God. In the Bible there simply are no casual meetings with God.

When my experience of intimacy with God is something akin to schmoozing with my best friend or produces the warm fuzzy feeling of a double martini, I have ended up with something less than the God of the Bible. That's idolatry. When my claims on intimacy with God become a substitute for healthy intimacy with other human beings, that's neurotic transference. When intimacy with God means assuming that God has the same concern I have for every detail of my narcissistic life, that is not only naive but is an expression of my sinfulness.

Frankly, I am sick of believers who talk so glibly and easily about "what the Lord is doing" and "what the Lord has revealed." It's as if they have God corralled. In the name of spiritual intimacy, some people have God so domesticated that there is no chance of falling down awestruck and speechless before One whose holiness threatens us to the core.

This attitude of self-indulgent intimacy with God is not only presumptuous. It is also blasphemous. The vague and remote God of the serious agnostic is more compatible with the God of the Bible, it seems to me, than the always-on-call, ingratiating, and even servile God of many true believers.

Moses once asked to see God's glory. God indicated that face-to-face intimacy was not possible: "For no one shall see me and live" (Exod 33:20). Moses was placed in the cleft of a rock and permitted to see only the backside of God's glory. It is clear in the Bible that overreaching in terms of intimacy with the holy things is deadly.

Yet the God of the Bible longs for intimacy with us. God is a lover who woos, who waits, who goes in search of, who becomes jealous, who weeps over faithless Israel as one betrayed. God, Jesus said, is like a father who wants intimacy with his two sons, one who is far away and one who is at home, but who knows that reciprocated love cannot be coerced. God knows us far more intimately than we know ourselves (Ps 139), and this knowledge is infinitely more gracious than our knowledge of ourselves. Yet God does not coerce or manipulate us, because love that is not freely given is not love.

Finally, therefore, prayer must take into account both God's transcendence and God's immanence. This means dealing with the ultimate interpersonal paradox, yet both dimensions of the reality of God must be acknowledged. When they are, prayer itself becomes paradoxical and can only be described in words that seem contradictory. For example, it's a strange phrase, but I would suggest that prayer aims at intimacy with the Mystery.

Prayer from God's Side

A large part of whatever I know about interpersonal relationships and/or intimacy I learned by years of adolescent observation. Since I found I liked girls but had no clue as to how to relate to them, I watched the other guys, especially the older ones. I saw that coming on too strong was usually counterproductive. A guy who moved in too quickly and easily on a girl, who inundated her with clever banter and even flattery assuming that she was going to be responsive, was usually disappointed. She felt overwhelmed, patronized, and manipulated. On the other hand, the boy who kept too much respectful distance, who admired from so far away as to be invisible, never made contact for lack of initiative. Girls can't read your mind, at least not until they know you.

I learned something that, like most important lessons, is easier to understand than to practice. The key, I found, is finding an appropriate balance between being respectful, being vulnerable, and being honest. As a naive male, I was surprised to find that what girls want at this point is exactly what boys want. We all want, and don't want, the same things. First, I don't want invasion. Even if I like you, I need you to respect my space and my personhood. When you make assumptions about my interest or affection, I feel used. My feeling is that you don't really care about me; it's all about you. I feel like prey. That throws me into a defensive, self-protective gear.

Second, I don't want aloofness. I may not want smothering, but I do want to know that you have some interest in me. So, take some appropriate risk with me. Push the door open a little from your side. Becoming vulnerable does not have to mean groveling, but it does mean revealing something of yourself.

Third, I don't want manipulation. Until I can trust you, we may have encounters, but we will have no relationship. Trust is based on truth. This is not truth as brutal honesty, which is usually destructive; this is truth as tender honesty, what St. Paul called "speaking the truth in love" (Eph 4:15). Feeling manipulated, especially by someone I hoped to trust, saddens me, angers me, turns me off, shuts me down. It frustrates the possibility of my giving to you what you say you want from me.

Have we jumped track? Wasn't this supposed to be about prayer? Are we learning how to pray here, or how to improve our personal relationships? Good question.

If we are made in the image of God, God must be at least as much a self or a person as we are. The supreme interpersonal relationship, then, would be with God, the eternal Thou. All other relationships are similar but derivative and secondary.

Learning to pray is not something as superficial as finding the correct formula or getting the words right. The proper posture of prayer is not that different from the posture we assume in any meaningful interpersonal relationship. If I am *imago Dei*, made in the image of God, then what I want in a relationship cannot be very different from what God wants in a relationship. If I am made in God's image, then I can see how God might want to be revered and respected as a unique self, instead of simply presumed upon, like a parent is by a small child. If I am made in God's image, then I can see how God might want us to be vulnerable, risking, not self-protective as if we had something to fear. If I am made in God's image, then I can see how God might want us to be honest, telling the whole truth and not just what sounds good. Now, apply those criteria to most of what we call prayer, and you may see why so much of it is so ineffectual.

In the reevaluation of all things that sometimes follows failure, nothing is more important than this: finding that reality has an intensely personal core, a center that is a Self, and finding that we are invited to approach this One as we would want to be approached ourselves by those we love most. Many books on prayer are popular because they are "how to" books, and people basically want to know how prayer "works." I hope you see why I would have trouble with a subject like "Making Prayer Work for You." I would have the same problem with a title like "How to Get Your Spouse to Do Everything You Want."

If God is a Thou, a Self in whose image we are made, then prayer is neither a strategy nor a tool, neither a quick fix nor an escape hatch. Prayer is interpersonal communication, or, even better, prayer is communion. We can no more plot the dialogue of prayer in advance for each other than we can give a bride and groom a script for their honeymoon. No relationship is predictable, and no two relationships are exactly alike. God wants a relationship with each one of us that is as unique as each one of us.

I only discovered that my parents were persons, or selves like me, when I was about thirteen and did something that hurt them badly. Always before, they had been there to take care of me, to meet my needs. But after this dark adolescent experience, I began to see that we were cut from the same mold. They could hurt the same way I hurt. They faced limitations and an uncertain future just as I did. And they needed respect, and affirmation, and love just as I did. It changed the way I saw them and gradually changed the way I related to them. It will change your world, I believe, if you can begin to understand prayer from God's side. Therefore, let us pray.

Note

[1]Harry Emerson Fosdick, *The Living of These Days* (New York: Harper & Row, 1956) 75.

The Inner Promised Land

Pick up the pieces,
let's see what's been broken,
What's become of us?
How do we manage to do so much damage
to the ones we love?
....
We raise our hopes, we dream our dreams,
and then we do some foolish thing.
But love that comes easy will easily give up.
When we fail love we've got to trust
the Love that won't fail us.

—Kyle Matthews
"When We Fail Love"

10

Light in Failure's Night

All of life, Myron Madden said once in my hearing, is lived somewhere between Egypt and the Promised Land. I am sure this extraordinary pastoral psychologist is correct, but the questions remain: What Egypt? What Promised Land?

The consequences of serious failure are far-reaching. They not only devastate the world around us, but they race into the future like storm troopers and destroy our promised lands.

The point of this book is to affirm that failure does not have to be the end. There can be life after failure. Still, the simplest honesty requires acknowledging the obvious, that failure is the end of some things. The inventory that follows failure always shows that some of our promised lands are missing.

Our promised lands define us. If I tell you what motivates my striving, if I tell you my goals and aspirations, my dreams, I will have told you much of who I am.

My promised land may be geographical. As a native son of the Lone Star state, I know a lot of transplanted Texans who live for nothing more intensely than getting back to Texas. My promised land may be a career goal, a certain amount of money, a certain degree of power, grandchildren, retirement, or relocation. "Oh, to be in England/Now that April's there." Where I want to go is a large part of who I am.

Believing in promised lands invariably requires imagination and idealism. Many young ministers scramble toward the promised land of an ideal church. We think, "Somewhere out there is the church of my destiny—large, prestigious, all of its members sophisticated and mature. Someday I will leave behind the pettiness and provincialism of this church, and I will go to a place where ministry is significant, stimulating, and fulfilling. Now, don't get me wrong. I love the *people* here; I just need more of a challenge."

The bad news is, of course, that there are no ideal churches. It takes some of us an entire career to figure that out. Meanwhile, congregations have to come to terms with another fact: There are no ideal ministers. The good news, on the other hand, is that the idealism and imagination involved in promised land aspirations may help motivate professional and personal growth in the young minister and may keep hope alive in the churches. Fantasies don't have to be realistic to be useful.

The point is, a large part of the meaning of my life lies in my promised lands. When they disappear, especially if I have some responsibility for their loss, my life suddenly may seem both meaningless and hopeless.

A Gift of the Darkness

My own moral failure, now over a decade ago, destroyed essentially all of the promised lands that mattered to me at that time. Both the grandeur and misery of the professional ministry is that it is life-absorbing. One's whole life is colored and shaped by this vocational calling. It is not merely that the world insists on seeing you in a stereotyped role that is difficult to shake off. It is that you yourself become immersed in such a significant and joyful sense of meaning and mission that all of your horizons become extensions of it. For twenty years I had not questioned my career choice or looked with envy at anyone else's job. All of my promised lands were connected, directly or indirectly, to what I knew was my life's work. In many professions a failure in one's personal life has little or no impact on one's working life. The same failure in a minister's life affects everything, and should.

It is very dark when even the backlighting of your horizons is gone. It becomes darker when your scurrying about produces no alternative horizons. For six months I couldn't find a job, much less a position in ministry. When I finally did, I still found no horizons in my life.

Some things, however, seem to be seen only in the dark. It is not uncommon for our artists and philosophers to refer back to some "dark night of the soul" as becoming a strange and unanticipated source of light.

Perhaps time and the aging process would have eventually brought me to the same conclusion, but for me it was a gradual epiphany that I see now as a gift of the darkness. It was the realization that the only promised land that ultimately matters is one my failure cannot destroy. It is the inner promised land of my completed self, my growing soul.

For some of us, it may be that only the loss of our external horizons can clarify the reality of our greater destiny. Success can be blinding and, in giving us the fruit of our striving, can steal our souls.

Canadian novelist Brian Moore finds failure a more interesting subject than success and, demonstrates this in his books. He once said:

> Success changes people. It makes them something they were not and dehumanizes them in a way, whereas failure leaves you with a more intense distillation of that self you are.[1]

Who Am I?

In a significant sense, the most serious human crisis is not to know who I am. I have never known anyone with an extended case of amnesia, but many writers have composed plots around what a horrifying predicament that would be. What could be worse than to be otherwise fully functional and not to know who I am? It is nightmare material.

Ours is the era of the "identity crisis." Erik Erikson is credited with having coined the term. His work, as clearly as anyone's, demonstrated how, amid all our drives and needs and neuroses, we must have some developing sense of who we are. This critical identity need distinguishes me from the ficus over in the corner. Find me with my identity structure in tact and all is well. Remove a couple of planks and all systems go haywire.

An expanding pluralism today makes an identity crisis almost inevitable. Once, when we lived in tribes, or families living together like tribes, or homogeneous communities, a relatively vivid sense of identity came with the territory. There were established rituals for imparting to and instilling in the child potent answers to the questions of origin, destiny, and identity. Identity crises were effectively headed off at the pass. That world is gone. The world of religious, ethnic, and cultural diversity, in elbow-to-elbow proximity is here. A child in a melting pot neighborhood such as the one I live in has a bewildering environment for finding an identity.

In social circles, and at the most practical level, everyone knows that the question of identity and the question of origin are inseparable. If you are interested in knowing who I am, one of the first questions you will ask me is where I come from. This is ancient wisdom. One's source defines one, if not exclusively, at least enough to let you know if you want to proceed toward a relationship.

The "s" at the end of my surname is an identification mark. Somewhere back in the dark forest of family trees it meant "son of Matthew." We don't know who the original Matthew was. My theory, or course, is that I am a direct descendant of the writer of the first Gospel. Some of us need rather desperately to believe in the exceptional significance of our origins.

Have you noticed that the most disparaging references we make to each other, as when one driver is muttering to another driver, involve slanderous dispersions on each other's origins? Think about it. The ultimate put-down is to impugn a person's parentage, and there is a veritable encyclopedia of degrading ammunition we have found useful in firing on one another's ancestors.

It is said that Alexander Dumas, the French writer, was asked by an antagonist, "Who was your father?" Dumas replied, "My father was a Creole, his father was a Negro, and his father a monkey. My family, it seems, begins where yours left off."

Maybe we have so much uncertainty about the identity question precisely because we are shaky and insecure about our origins. If we begin with no clear sense of who we are, we look to our environment to tell us. Out there something or someone puts a spin on most of the information we receive about ourselves and our origins, and the net result is bad news to us.

You thought you looked ok, and then the kids at school started making fun of your clothes. You liked your house, and then a friend said it sure was small. You were proud of your church, and then you heard someone say, "Boy, the people who go there are really strange."

The tendency to feel bad about ourselves gets established early. Thereafter, all of our experiences of failure seem to confirm those feelings.

The stories of how we have sought to resolve our identity crises are more pathetic than inspirational. The drive to know who we are, or to distinguish ourselves as someone, leads to some of the silliest and most destructive things we do. We get bizarre with our hair and wear shocking outfits in an attempt to find out who we are. We marry in search of an identity. We divorce in search of an identity. We use and abuse people in search of an identity. When someone says, "I need to find myself," we have learned to get ready for anything.

We go to school forever trying to find ourselves, or we drop out of school trying to find ourselves. We enter a profession that promises an identity. God only knows how many have entered the ministry for that reason. We keep believing that somewhere there is a title that will tell us who we are.

We join political organizations feeling that identification with a cause is the same as an identity. We study horoscopes, sign up for self-help programs, or join some sectarian religion, and just let some authoritarian person tell us who we are. Still, too many of us go to our graves like Willy Loman, not knowing who we are.

First Love

The creation narratives of the book of Genesis frame every question that matters about our origins. If Genesis does not give you all the answers you want, it will certainly introduce you to the right questions, which is infinitely more important. You can't find the right answers if you aren't asking the right questions.

Most of the Bible is about salvation or redemption, you say, not about creation. But that redemption cannot be understood accept in the light of creation. Redemption? Redemption *from* what? Redemption *to* what? The answers are in the Bible's understanding of creation.

Creation is good. It is exactly what God had in mind. Redemption is simply God's work to restore creation. The creature made in God's image and given freedom has made selfish and destructive choices. In our fall, we have brought creation down with us. The God of love patiently works at re-creation.

The good news we find in the story of creation is that we have our origins, and therefore, our identity, in the eternal love of God. Your life is not simply "the outcome of accidental collocations of atoms," as Bertrand Russell said.[2] You were born in love. We are God's children now, and what that leads to is not even within our range of vision (1 John 3:2). We love because God first loved us (1 John 4:19).

Your first love was not the little red-haired girl in elementary school. Your first love was not the awkward boy who first made your heart go pitty-pat. Your first love was the God who created you in love.

Did you think it was only after you were created that God decided whether to love you or not? Most of the theologians have known better. They say that God loved us and, therefore, created us. They say it was love that moved God to give us existence. That's a pretty high recommendation. If it is true, what an identity you have. Look where you are from, child of God, created in love. In the real world, however, isn't it too incredible to be true? Can such origins in love actually be the story of any person's life?

Yesterday I became a grandfather for the first time. Everyone tells me, of course, that I don't look old enough to be a grandfather, and I believe them. Emily Grace Matthews—I have not even seen her yet. One thing I know, however, is that she is a creation of love. I know her parents, in some ways better than they know themselves (at least one of them). They loved the idea of her even during the years when they were not sure they could have a child. The suggestion that, when they saw her for the first time yesterday, they looked at her to see if they loved her would be absurd.

A decade ago my sister and brother-in-law adopted a baby after their own years of trying without success to conceive. They named her Rachel Bond. Since then they have adopted Rebecca, too. When Rachel was old enough to appreciate books and stories, and ask questions, my sister, Kay, created for her the story of her origins in pictures and words. What is clear in that very honest story is that Rachel, too, was loved before she was born.

Have you heard the story of your origins? It is the story of who you are. You are created in the very image of the One who made you. You are God's child. Deny it or distort it through your moral failures, but it is your true and unchanging identity.

All of life is lived between Egypt and the Promised Land. That means in the wilderness. Egypt we know. The wilderness we know. But what Promised Land? The Creator's greatest desire for you is that you might claim your birthright, that you might begin living, even in the wilderness, in the joyful knowledge of who you are, and that you might follow that light all the way home.

Notes

[1]Quoted in *The New Yorker*, 15 July 1996, 78.

[2]Bertrand Russell, "A Free Man's Worship," *The Basic Writings of Bertrand Russell, 1903–1959*, ed. Robert E. Egner and Lester E. Denonn (New York: Simon & Schuster, 1961) 67.

11

The Great Invitation

Some of the best things and some of the worst things that happen to us are the result of accepting invitations. You accept one person's invitation to dinner, and it becomes one of the most memorable evenings of your life. You accept another person's invitation, and it develops into an evening of agony. You respond to this opportunity to buy or invest, and it pays off. You go for another nice-looking offer, and you lose everything. It would certainly make living easier if we could see in advance the consequences of saying yes.

Still, it's nice to be invited. It makes us feel important, included, wanted. Most of us work with just enough insecurity that we have difficulty turning down any invitation. We pay for this with a diffused existence, our lives delivered in all directions at once. However that may be, we could all write a fairly extensive autobiography simply in terms of the invitations we have accepted.

For me, one invitation overshadows the rest. It is the invitation of Jesus. I have found it to be the great invitation in comparison to which all other invitations pale.

The Gospel writers show Jesus at the beginning of his ministry inviting common fishermen to follow him. What prepared them for this response we don't know, but Peter, Andrew, James, and John immediately dropped their nets and went with him.

The invitation was always there in Jesus' life. Look closely, and you will see that all his encounters were charged with the dynamics of calling, beckoning, inviting. The people of first-century Palestine invariably found in him something new, a new challenge, a new possibility. Some were enchanted and followed eagerly. Others were threatened and began setting traps. But there were few casual meetings with Jesus.

"Lazarus, come forth!" was essentially what Jesus said to every person. "Leave the deadness of where you are, and come to the aliveness of where I am."

Jesus calls us away from wherever we are. If we are up a tree, he calls us down and goes home with us. If we are at home, he calls us to the ends of the earth. If we are in the place of conflict, he calls us to the place of peace. If we are in the place of peace he calls us to the place of conflict. He is the inviting One. Poet W. H. Auden wrote:

> He is the Way.
> Follow Him through the Land of Unlikeness;
> You will see rare beasts and have unique adventures.[1]

The new is threatening, however. The dimension of the unknown, even in the invitation of Jesus, unsettles us and makes us hesitant.

In the British Museum in London you can observe something of the history of cartography, the science of mapmaking. Some of the maps there are reported to be more than four thousand years old. I was intrigued by the way ancient mapmakers represented the unexplored, unknown areas of their world. They would fill these regions with depictions of dragons, monsters, and other threatening creatures. Our tendency is to approach the unknown with the most negative imaginings. We associate light and security with the known, but darkness and threat with the unknown.

Yet we are always facing something unknown. Living means coping with the ever-emerging new: the new school or job, the new relationship or requirement, the new freedom or limitation. Do you remember the first time someone offered you a raw oyster? We often cringe at the prospect of the new. It is not just this unknown aspect that makes the new threatening, however. The new usually means the loss of something old, something familiar, something loved.

The day my parents left me at college, I was a bundle of conflicting emotions. I stood there in front of the dorm, wearing my freshman "slime cap," and watched my childhood being driven away in the car with my parents. I had both an exhilirating sense of freedom and a disturbing sense of loss. Part of me wanted to be a little boy going back home with them.

The invitation of Jesus is the great invitation not because there are no threats. Jesus made it clear that following him involves all manner of uncertainty. It could mean facing something unwanted, and it could mean losing something that matters. This is the great invitation, not because it is not threatening, but because what it offers is worth the risk.

What does it offer? Heaven? Eternal life? Yes, that promise is there. But life after death is not the first thing to which we are invited, and certainly not the only thing. Because God is in the business of creation and redemption, the invitation of Jesus is the beckoning to become who we really are.

In Bible books such as Genesis and Romans, we see that sin is not simply breaking rules and laws. Sin is failing to be who God created us to be. It is missing the mark. We have thought, or been taught, that sin reflects our true selves. "When I sin, that is the real me," we have said. Quite the opposite is true. When I sin, I am failing to be the "real me."

Here is the ancient image that holds the first clue to your true identity. The Creator shapes you from the clay of the earth, breathes life into you, inspects you, and pronounces you good. You, as God makes you, are good. The "real you" is good. Sin is whatever keeps you from being who and what God created you to be.

Those first followers, the fishermen, responded to what seemed a very obscure invitation. What happened is that these ordinary, even unlikely people began to become who they really were.

Ernest Campbell once delivered a first-person narrative, as if he were Simon Peter. Part of it went something like this. "Jesus said, 'Who do the people say I am? Who do you say I am?' I said, 'You are the Christ.' Jesus said, 'You are Peter.' How wondrously strange and how much more than coincidence that when I told him who he was I learned who I was, too." God created Simon to be a rock. But it took the great invitation for that to be realized.

Can you hear what this means for you? It means that as a creation of God you are beautiful and good. You can stop your self-deprecating, your self-despising. It is not necessary to punish yourself. The invitation of Jesus is not to become less of what you are, but more of what you truly are. This is why it is the great invitation. It offers you not only God; it offers you yourself.

In Truman Capote's *Other Voices, Other Rooms* there is a character called "Zoo." Her real name is Missouri, and she is the granddaughter of an old black preacher she calls Papadaddy. The novel's main character is Joel, a white boy. "I'm thirteen," he declares. "And you'd be suprised how much I know." Zoo responds, "Shoot, boy, the country's just fulla folks what knows everythin, and don't unnerstand nothin, just fullofem."[2] Though some think she's crazy, she personifies the largely indescribable quality of the person who is real, the person who is authentic.

The most beautiful people I have known have not necessarily been physically attractive. That cherished gift is brief and fleeting, and before long gravity pulls all of us out of shape. The most beautiful people I have known have not necessarily been intelligent. "Knows everythin, and don't unnerstand nothin." The most beautiful people I have known are those rarities who know themselves. They are those who, usually in knowing they are accepted by God, have accepted themselves. They are real, believable, alive. This, I think, makes them like Jesus.

I see Jesus as the most thoroughly real person who ever lived. His life resounds with the ring of truth. Pure quality, complete authenticity—he defines integrity. He invites us to begin the adventure of becoming real. This is the great invitation.

Let there be no misleading, no deception, no hearing of false claims. Much popular religion makes promises it cannot deliver. The invitation of Jesus can be twisted into an appeal to our lower natures, to our avarice and self-centeredness. It amounts to suggesting that we can set the agenda and Jesus will work for us. It dresses mammon in Christian garb, plays on our gullibility and desperation, and calls this darkness light.

Do you remember the temptation experience of Jesus in the wilderness? It was a time of testing and of Jesus determining what kind of Messiah he would be. I respectfully submit that much popular Christianity has unconsciously succumbed to every temptation Jesus rejected. Jesus does not invite us to a quick fix, but to a following; not to worldly power, but to the spiritual power of love; not to instant peace, but to a pilgrimage. God's agenda is so different from ours that often, in the words of Miguel de Unamuno, God may deny us peace to give us glory.

Can you hear Jesus say that if we would follow him we must take up crosses and still believe that Jesus wants whatever we want? When we do a reconstruction job on Jesus' invitation and make it what we want it to be, then we make it something other than the great invitation.

What, therefore, does it mean to follow Jesus? It would be presumptuous to try to say it all. The answers are probably as many and as varied as the followers. Still, wouldn't following Jesus at least mean letting him show us how to think of God? Wouldn't following Jesus at least mean listening seriously to his primary claim, that seeking the kingdom of God, as clearly distinguished from all other kingdoms, is life's most critical issue?

Wouldn't following Jesus at least mean letting him set the agenda for our lives? Wouldn't it at least mean coming to grips with his claim that losing one's life is the way of finding one's life? Wouldn't it at least mean not assuming that we know where he is going?

Following Jesus means tossing our own itineraries and letting him lead us in directions we have never considered. What else could he have possibly meant when he said, "Whoever loves father or mother more than me is not worthy of me" (Matt 10:37)? This is no field trip to which Jesus invites us. It is an enlistment. Where will we find courage for this following, this cross bearing? Who can pay this cost of discipleship? How do we rise to its challenge?

With the great invitation comes a great promise. It is the promise of an accompanying presence. Jesus says, "I am with you always" (Matt 28:20). The threatening way becomes viable because the One who invites us also goes with us. The God of the Bible is not just a God of invitation, but a God of promise. "As your days, so is your strength" (Deut 33:25).

In *The Hiding Place*, Corrie ten Boom tells of confronting death for the first time as a child. The death of an infant forces on her the realization that death will someday come to everyone, even those she loves most.

> Still shivering with that cold, I followed Nollie up to our room and crept into bed beside her. At last we heard Father's footsteps winding up the stairs. It was the best moment in every day, when he came to tuck us in. . . . But that night as he stepped through the door I burst into tears. "I need you!" I sobbed. "You can't die! You can't!" . . . Father sat down on the edge of the narrow bed. "Corrie," he began gently, "when you and I go to Amsterdam, when do I give you your ticket?" I sniffed a few times, considering this. "Why, just before we get on the train." "Exactly. And our wise Father in heaven knows when we're going to need things, too. Don't run out ahead of Him, Corrie. When the time comes that some of us will have to die, you will look into your heart and find the strength you need—just in time."[3]

The great invitation and a great promise. "As your days, so is your strength." As in that long-ago time when he called common people into an uncommon adventure, even so, in our confusing age, Jesus says, "Come and see. Follow me."

Notes

[1]W. H. Auden, "For the Time Being, A Christmas Oratorio," *W. H. Auden, Collected Poems*, ed. Edward Mendelson (New York: Vintage Books, 1976) 400.

[2]Truman Capote, *Other Voices, Other Rooms* (New York: Random House, 1948) 56.

[3]Corrie ten Boom, *The Hiding Place* (New York: Bantam Books, 1971) 29.

12

Faith for the Journey

In the summer of 1975, while spending a month in Hawaii (doing ministry, of course), I read James Michener's novel, Hawaii. The first section of the book is Michener's version of how the first humans came to the islands, and it suggests one of the most incredible journeys ever made.

In the ninth century, a group of Polynesians were forced to leave their home on the island of Bora Bora in the south Pacific. On a double canoe, large enough to accommodate fifty people, they started north across a vast, uncharted ocean. They had no assurance that anything awaited them but this infinity of water. Legend had it that somewhere to the north, beneath a formation of stars called the Seven Little Eyes, there was a land that would sustain them. But it was only a legend.

They traveled nearly 5,000 miles, at sea approximately a month, suffering every imaginable hardship. They made this unbelievable voyage at a time when ships in Europe and Asia seldom sailed out of view of land.

Where does the courage come from for such a journey? For the Bora Borans, it came from the fact that they carried their gods with them. Safely housed on board, given more protection even than the king, were their deities. They sailed with a simple logic: Our gods are with us; therefore, we will not be afraid.

Does this mean that, despite all their life-and-death ordeals, it was actually easier back then? How convenient to have your gods where you can see them, and how comforting to have your gods involved in every aspect of your journey. Since all human journeys are in some sense ventures into the unknown, they all require some kind of faith. Maybe it is simply faith in ourselves, or in our tribe, or in good fortune, but we always proceed in faith.

What kind of faith is appropriate for the endeavor being encouraged here, the journey toward the inner promised land? If we undertake this inward expedition, with what confidence can we begin?

Romans 8:28a (KJV)

In human crises of every kind Christians for generations have both offered comfort and sought it in the familiar phrase from Romans 8:28: "All things work together for good." There may be no satisfactory explanation for why, in a world in which God is sovereign, a child dies from an esoteric disease, or a young person bright with promise is killed in a car wreck, or a tornado destroys a home. So some well-intentioned believer will say, "We don't know why this terrible thing has happened, but we know that 'all things work together for good.' "

If I could have articulated my philosophy of life when I was a baby, I might have used this phrase. It would have been easy for me to believe as an infant or a small child that the world around me was organized primarily for my benefit. My needs were quickly met with almost no effort on my part. I was the center of the universe, and everything and everyone orbited around me. When I was six years old, however, a terrible thing happened. I was forced to go to first grade. Almost immediately I began to discover that all things did not work together for good, at least not for my good. The first day of school I had the most embarrassing experience of my life. Because I didn't know where the restroom was, I didn't get there in time. My mother had dressed me in green corduroys, which to my everlasting shame revealed everything.

During those first weeks of school, I accidentally swallowed a penny on the school bus. Pennies had value back then. I was holding the penny between my teeth while I arranged all the stuff I was taking home when suddenly the bus bolted, and I swallowed the coin. Since I had not had biology, I assumed that if you swallowed a penny you died. So I began to act like a dying person, and my peers gathered around to watch. The wise bus driver, who apparently had studied biology, assured me that I would not die, and that in fact I would live to see that penny again. It was good news, but did little to help my humiliation.

Also during that first-grade year I had a serious accident on the playground. I bear the scar on my left leg to this day.

I was beginning to learn what my life has confirmed ever since, that all things don't work together for good. This, after all, is not faith, but belief in fate. It is presumptuous and naive in the assumption that the universe is ultimately organized with me in mind. I assure you it is not. All things don't work together for good.

Romans 8:28 (complete, KJV)

A second look, of course, clearly shows that Romans 8:28 does not claim that "all things work together for good." If you read the entire verse, you read: "For we know that all things work together for good to them that love God, to them who are the called according to his purpose."

Aha! The biblical claim is not that "all things work together for good" for everybody, but for those people who "love God" and are "called according to his purpose." That made sense. If you are good, God will treat you good. I made a decided move in the direction of those people.

I found, however, that even when I was loving God most and serving God best, bad things still happened to me. Adolescence, in case you have forgotten, is a little piece of hades. This is when, in the words of the Janis Ian song, we know "the pain of valentines that never came," and of having our names "never called when choosing sides for basketball." Loving and serving God didn't seem to have any appreciable effect on my adolescent experiences of rejection and failure.

Then I discovered that this was not just an adolescent problem. As a young adult I found that some of the people whom I knew loved God most and served God best still experienced suffering and failure. When my own mother died of breast cancer at age 63, in many ways in the prime of her life, I knew that all things don't work together for good even for those who love God most and serve God best.

It was a grim but vital lesson for me. I must not base my faith on what happens to me and to those I love. God "makes his sun rise on the evil and on the good, and sends rain on the righteous and on the unrighteous" (Matt 5:45). Faith is not the belief that God practices favoritism. No matter how much you love God, you're going to get hurt, and you're going to lose something that matters, and someone you love is going to die.

It is my solid conviction that neither of the readings of Romans 8:28 we have considered can withstand either honest reflection or the bright light of reality. The first reading turns faith into a naive belief in fate, and the second makes faith an equally naive belief in divine favoritism.

Faith is something deeper and worthier. Ironically, a key to a more viable faith can be found in the very verse that seems to have withered before us.

Romans 8:28-29 (RSV, NEB, TEV, et al)

For all the beauty of the Elizabethan English of the King James Version, it can be confusing to American readers four centuries later. Also, most Bible scholars agree that it is not the most technically accurate translation from the Hebrew and Greek. In most modern translations of the Bible you will not find the phrase, "all things work together for good."

Furthermore, as useful as it is to have the Bible divided into numbered chapters and verses, this is not the way the material was written. Since the Geneva Bible of 1560, we have been able to find our way through the Bible by means of this numbering system, but we have also come to think of the Bible as a book of verses, as being comprised of isolated little units that can be read by themselves without reference to their context.

Reading it in a more recent translation and seeing it in its context brought Romans 8:28 to life for me and keeps providing light. This verse does not say "all things work together for good," but "in everything God works for good with those who love him, who are called according to his purpose" (RSV). The subject of the sentence is God. Everything that happens is not the will of God, but God is at work in everything that happens to bring good out of it.

What is the good for which God works? We all know what is good, don't we? Health is good. Success is good. Prosperity is good. Pleasure is good.

Many people believe that this is the good for which God works. However, the verse that follows verse 28 makes clear that the good for which God works is that we might "be conformed to the image of his Son." Don't be put off by the verb "predestined." It simply means that God determined before creation that Jesus Christ would be the pattern and goal of our humanity. God was predisposed in eternity to work in all things for the supreme good of making us like Jesus.

Of course things happen in my life that are unpleasant, even seriously threatening. But there is nothing that happens to me that does not have redemptive potential, that God cannot use to make me more like Jesus. Sometimes, in fact, something most painful to me may be most useful to God. The miracle of resurrection occurs only when something or someone has died.

Romans 8:28-29 (verified)

L. D. Johnson personified faith as much as anyone I have known. His was not an easy faith, but a tested faith that was a realistic and creative struggle. It showed physically. He looked like an Old Testament prophet. He had the demeanor of someone who had survived an impossible journey, but whom the ordeal had left exceptionally wise. And that is what he was.

He died during Christmas of 1981. A whole city grieved, those who had known him as a pastor, those who had known him as a university chaplain, those who read his weekly columns in the newspaper. It was my privilege and dreaded responsibility to officiate at his service. He had suffered terribly before he died. After all he had endured in life, he deserved a better end.

He had grown up an orphan in Oklahoma. A brother stayed home to work so he could go to college. He was a superb scholar and seemed destined to both effectiveness and struggle. He and Marion had four children. A son died in infancy. A daughter was killed as a young adult in an automobile accident. A grown son, a minister, died in 1996 after a lifetime of fragile health. One daughter, Elaine, remains. Marion Johnson has seen a husband and three children enter the valley of the shadow of death.

L. D. was harrassed in the 1960s as a southern pastor who took a stand on civil rights. Then, during many of his fertile university chaplaincy years, he was distracted by health concerns.

Some time during his last years, he taught the book of Romans at a church in Virginia. The pastor of the church, Vernon Davis, says that when L. D. came to Romans 8:28-30, it was late one evening. L. D. said, "I can document from personal experience that these words are true, but it would be painful for me, and it would take more time than we have tonight. Let me assure you, however, that I know these words are true."

Davis said, "That is the kind of person whom I want to tell me about those words. . . . Not someone who has never had to depend upon them because life has treated them kindly. Not someone who has experienced pain and suffering and become cynical because of it. I want to listen to one who has in the midst of the darkness of suffering honestly sought after God and that possibility of salvation and found it."

A picture of L. D. Johnson hangs on the wall of my office directly in front of me when I sit at my computer. He looks down on my work. I've often wondered what he would say to me about my failure. Moral failure was especially distasteful to this courageous man. Ten years ago my shame almost kept me from putting the picture on my wall. I knew L. D. would be disappointed in me. And I knew he would never say, "It's o.k. What you did doesn't matter." The picture is on my wall because I decided how L. D. would respond. I think he might say, "In all things God works for good . . . even in your failure. Go forward in this faith."

God with Us

Faith for the inward journey is not sight. Even if we believe that the inner promised land is a selfhood like that of Jesus, we still go forward in darkness concerning what that will mean. The destination remains vague, because "no eye has seen, nor ear heard, nor the human heart conceived, what God has prepared for those who love him" (1 Cor 2:9).

Our faith is not in the destination, especially not as we might imagine it, but in the God who goes with us. Our faith is in the God who loves us and who is at work in all things for a good beyond our comprehension. Faith is not sight.

A young woman had to be rushed to the hospital. The doctor said she would need to stay overnight for more tests, and told her husband and their small son to go home and come back the next day. The house was dark and seemed very empty. "Daddy, can I sleep with you?" Lying in bed, they both struggled quietly with their apprehension. Finally, the boy spoke.

"Daddy, is your face turned toward me?" "Yes, son, it is; now go to sleep." When the boy was asleep the father got up and walked to the bedroom window. Outside it seemed utterly, endlessly dark. After a moment he whispered, "Father, is your face turned toward me?"

It is. When we experience it, and when we don't, God is for us and with us. Brave journey!

13

The Gift of Adequacy

As the Good Shepherd turned his sheep out into the wild wolf-country of the world, he said, "Do not worry about how you are to speak or what you are to say; for what you are to say will be given to you" (Matt 10:19). I find, however, even when there are no wolves present, it is difficult to be free from anxiety about how to speak and what to say. This is especially true if you have the audacity to try to speak for God.

We preachers, when we have preached, are always anxious to find out how we did. So we go stand in some vulnerable place, such as the front door of the church, where people can tell us how we did. Or, considerably more risky, we ask our spouses when we get home.

A certain minister was driving home from church one Sunday still a little high from preaching. He mused to his wife, "You know, there aren't many truly great preachers left in this country." She replied, "You are right, and there is even one less than you think."

George Buttrick used to tell of a woman who, as she was leaving church one Sunday, shook his hand and said, "I'll say, Dr. Buttrick, I believe every sermon you preach is better than the next one!" Dr. Buttrick said he wondered if he should quit while he was ahead, because you can lose ground fast like that.

One of my former pastors, J. P. Allen, tells of a timid white-haired lady who came to him in the narthex and said earnestly, "Dr. Allen, I can't tell you how much your sermons have meant to my husband since he lost his mind."

We preachers listen to what people say about our preaching and keep hoping for the best. People are usually more gracious than we deserve. While I have heard some strange comments after preaching, and been corrected more than once, generally I have found encouragement, often in words that meant far more to me than the speaker could have imagined.

The strangest comment I ever received after preaching was spoken at one of the most important and sensitive times in my life. It was Senior Preaching Week at the seminary, and I was one of four students chosen to preach in chapel that week. Do I need to explain what a huge event that was in my life? It was both the most exhilarating and the most intimidating preaching situation I had ever faced. Generations of great preachers had stood in that pulpit. The congregation was made up largely of my peers, fellow students, with whom I competed for grades, for honors, and for the better churches. And they were sitting there looking, at least to me, like they knew they could do better. Worse, the faculty was there—my professors! I worked harder on that sermon than any three other sermons I have ever prepared.

When it was over, I felt good about it. It was a stressful but unforgettable experience. The comments made to me after the service, from both students and professors, reinforced that good feeling. I saw Dr. Hendricks waiting in line to speak to me. The next fall I was to become Dr. Hendricks' grader, and he was to be my major professor in the doctoral program. I cared more about what he thought than anybody else. He shook my hand. I waited for the blessing. With a characteristic lifting of one eyebrow, he said quietly, "David, that was adequate."

Adequate? How do you respond to that? I mumbled, "Thank you," and then wondered if that was appropriate. I was devastated. I had wanted to be great, and I was adequate.

One day that next fall I slipped into the back of one of Dr. Hendricks' undergraduate classes, because I was to teach the class the following week in his absence. When I sat down he had departed from the theology lecture and was lambasting the culture in general and preachers in particular for our terrible addiction to hyperbole, overstatement, and excessive use of superlatives. Our expressions of praise become meaningless, he said, because our superlatives have been used too many times when they shouldn't have been. He said we needed to re-examine the word "adequate." There was that word! "Consider the word 'adequate,' he said, "because adequate is as good as any of us ever needs to be." My teacher was teaching me.

What status does the word "adequate" have in your vocabulary? It probably falls in the category of gray words, bland words. Maybe it is for you a synonym for lukewarm. I once saw an actor in Sante Fe do a comic routine in which he played a bumbling magician. The magician's name was "Peter the Adequate."

I will confess, my secret ambition has always been to be great. When I was growing up, I wanted to be a lot of different things at different times, but I always wanted to be great. The biographies I read were not about ordinary people. They were about great people. I got the idea early that if I wasn't great, I wasn't anything.

Nothing will throttle that kind of ambition more quickly or thoroughly than serious conspicuous failure. In fact, the spectrum of history's judgment on individual lives runs precisely from greatness at one end to failure at the other. In the public mind the two concepts are mutually exclusive.

I have been in a long adult process of discovering that God's purposes and my ambitions are not always compatible. If you will run a check on what might be considered the words of promise in the Bible, I think you will find that God's promises have more to do with adequacy than with greatness.

I have also been learning that God's promises are more in tune with my true needs than my ambitions are. It is as though God, my supreme teacher, were saying, "Reconsider the word adequate, because 'adequate' is as good as you ever really need to be."

According to my dictionary, adequate means "sufficient for a specific requirement." My vanity aside, what more do I need for the adventure of living than to be "sufficient for a specific requirement"? Adequate really is as good as I ever need to be. Take, for example, the three major preoccupations of my life: my relationships, my work, and my personal struggles.

As I think of all the people I truly love, I ask, "What does genuine love require?" Certainly not greatness. Especially not greatness if that implies superiority or achievements in competition. Genuine love has no need for it and no place for it. What does love require? Adequacy—this only. I need to be adequate in accepting love, and I need to be adequate in giving love. God knows that in such a time as ours, aspiring to be an adequate husband or father or friend is no small aspiration.

My work is ministry, but that does not keep it from being work. The temptation to pursue greatness and success in one's work is no greater anywhere than in the professional ministry. We are about as busy climbing as anyone. But my growing experience is that ministry, like anything else, requires adequate workers and has little need of great workers. When you have helped meet a simple but serious need, when you have been privileged to speak a word of grace, when someone comes to you and finds the strength to go on a little longer, what more could you possibly need? Do you need this one whom you have been privileged to serve to fall down and worship you? Do you need an audience to applaud? The only thing that matters in the Kingdom of God is whether you are adequate in "speaking the truth in love" and in distributing the bread of life.

It is true, too, with regard to my personal struggles. The private, secret load gets so heavy sometimes, doesn't it? And the longer you are a burden bearer, the less you pray to be a hero, and the more you pray for sufficiency. Adequacy. There is a spiritual that says, "I don't want you to move the mountain, Lord; just give me grace to climb."

In the areas of my life that really matter, adequacy is what I need. And, by the grace of God, adequacy is what I am promised.

I have a private interpretation of the creation narratives in Genesis. I hope you have some private interpretations of parts of Scripture, too. I believe Adam and Eve fell into sin because, while they were promised adequacy, they reached for greatness. God gave them an appropriate place in the scheme of things, an impressive place, as God's caretakers of creation. But they could not accept their God-given humanity or God's promise to give them all they needed in fulfilling the divine will. They wanted more than they needed. Being adequate was not enough.

The gift of adequacy is usually experienced serendipitously. Here you are, set over against a situation that threatens to destroy you. Here you are, bending under a weight of circumstances that is about to break you. Here you are, struggling through some valley of death flanked by people leaning toward you for a word of life. And suddenly you begin to sense resources within you that you honestly did not know were there. Perhaps they weren't.

Most of us have been privileged to know at least a few people who achieved some measure of greatness. I have known my share. They are my models, some because they are centered and know who they are, some because they have become deep wells of wisdom the hard way, some because of their creative effort to offer something worthy to God and the world, some because they have led by serving, some because they exercised to my joy their gift for living joyfully, and some because they incarnated the love of God without knowing it. I have known other kinds of greatness that bordered on genius, those whose music spoke as words never can of transcendent things, those whose facility with words became a vehicle of the Word, those possessed of such understanding and discernment as to give a third dimension to my flat perceptions of truth.

None of these pursued greatness where they achieved it. It is a ludicrous suggestion. It is precisely because they sought to be adequate with regard to something they found to be more important than themselves that they achieved a greatness they cared little about. Invariably such people do not take themselves too seriously. Their focus is not on themselves.

My daughter, Keri, is a third-year seminary student in Richmond, Virginia. Since I was in seminary forever, it gives us a lot to talk about. I am going to seminary again vicariously through her, and it's much easier this way. However, while Keri is preparing for ministry, she is not following in her father's footsteps.

My seminary years were filled with ambition. Hers are not. My need was to achieve and excel. Hers is not. Keri does not even know what shape her ministry will take and is not anxious about it. This is not simply because the ministry has been so male-oriented that there is little room for female ambition. Keri and I both know some very ambitious women in the ministry. It is also not because she is exceptionally self-confident. I have watched her struggle with the same insecurities as everyone else, and she entered seminary in fear and trembling. It is because somewhere along the line Keri decided to be herself and to trust God to make that adequate.

I wonder where I'd be today if, when I was her age, I'd been where she is now. The road not taken. Did I set myself up for failure by being so afraid of failing? Is the desire for greatness always the prelude to sin?

Hear again Jesus' words to his disciples:

See, I am sending you out like sheep into the midst of wolves; . . . they will hand you over to councils and flog you in their synagogues; and you will be dragged before governors and kings because of me. . . . When they hand you over, do not worry about how you are to speak or what you are to say; for what you are to say will be given to you at that time; for it is not you who speak, but the Spirit of your Father speaking through you. (Matt 10:16-20)

We like the security of stored-up resources: a full stock of faith in advance; a mind that has it all figured out, with ready answers for any questions; money in the bank. The most effective servants of the Great Kingdom, however, have generally traveled light, sometimes only on a wing and a prayer and in their hearts a magnificent promise. It is the promise that in the hour of our extremity and need there is "extreme unction," grace, sufficiency, adequacy. Who in the serious business of living and loving and serving God could want more?

14

Seeing Beyond Our Living

During our earliest years of reading and moviegoing, most of us not only came to like but to expect happy endings. A given story might be full of conflicts, injustices, tragedies, even spine-tingling horror, but if there was happiness at the end, everything was all right. Past all wars, broken hearts, runaway children, and lost dogs, if there was a happy ending, we could close the book or leave the theater with a sense of satisfaction. Who doesn't like a story that leaves us feeling good?

We operate on a principle here: It's not so much what happens in the process that matters; it's how it ends. Life is worth living if, in the end, good triumphs, justice is done, and love conquers.

The story of Moses is one of the most interesting and dramatic stories, not just in the Old Testament, but anywhere. Born to a Hebrew peasant woman, Moses, through a remarkable series of events, came to be reared as an Egyptian prince. That's a pretty good story in itself. But as Moses gained prominence, his sympathies also grew for the plight of his people who were slaves in Egypt. One day in a burst of rage he killed an Egyptian he saw mistreating a Hebrew. Moses became a fugitive from Egyptian justice and a wilderness shepherd. To Moses' utter surprise, however, God found him in the wilderness and sent him to be the deliverer of his people from their bondage to Pharaoh.

The figure of Moses dominates the Old Testament. Something of his shadow falls across every page. In the Exodus, Israel's most defining event, Moses was the human bridge between the land of bondage and the land of promise. This half-century saga, with its principle character, Moses, has all the ingredients of the great story.

How disappointing, then, to come to the end of the story of Moses and find that it does not have the ending we want. Read it to its conclusion and you discover that, of all things, Moses never entered the Promised Land with the children of Israel.

How monumentally unfair. Moses died in the mountains of Moab, just across the Jordan River from the land to which he had led his people. To make it harder to take, it was God who closed the door. God kept Moses from crossing the Jordan, and the reasons are not at all easy to understand.

There is a bittersweet piece of consolation in the story. God does permit Moses to *see* the Promised Land. In what must have been the most poignant moment of his great life, Moses stood on Mount Nebo, near the top of Pisgah, and took the land of Canaan into his heart through his eyes.

The point at which most visitors today stand on Mount Nebo is some 4,000 feet above the Dead Sea, 2,700 feet directly above the city of Jericho. Looking to the left, the south, you see the north end of the Dead Sea, and on a clear day as far as Ein Gedi. Directly below is the vast valley of the Jordan River, the most visible city being Jericho, "the city of palm trees." Far to the north, under extremely favorable conditions, some have seen snow-capped Mount Hermon. Letting your eyes move south, you can see Mount Tabor, Mounts Ebal and Gerizim, the highlands of Judea, and the ridge running south toward Bethlehem and Hebron.

The one time I stood there was at the end of the day, at dusk. I could still see the mountain horizon to the west, a perfect backdrop for the lights coming on in distant Jerusalem, as well as down below in Jericho. It was a breathtaking sight. I tried to imagine the fullness of that moment for Moses.

Unfolded out before him was the promise of God. Here was the land on which he and his people had pinned all their hopes and dreams. All of this, this was home. This was the future.

Moses would die in those mountains on the wrong side of the Jordan River. But from Mount Nebo he had a panoramic view of the future. In that transcendent moment, Moses was seeing beyond his living.

The Practical Necessity

Perhaps the ending of the story of Moses isn't as tragic or as disappointing as it seems. Of course we would prefer to have the story end with Moses' weary feet standing on the western shore of the Jordan. At least we would prefer to have him buried in the Promised Land, properly enshrined in the land of his people's destiny, instead of hidden, lost somewhere in the mountains of Moab. But who gets to finish everything? Who gets to do it all? Who gets to live all the way to the end of the story?

Life is brief and bounded by limits. One person's life is a miniscule fraction of an inch on the road of history's many miles. "What is your life?" asked James. "You are a mist that appears for a little while and then vanishes" (Jas 4:14). One lifetime isn't much as we measure time. Why, when Moses looked down on Jericho from Mount Nebo, that city had already been in business for six thousand years!

Some of our lifetimes will not even reach the average. A number of years ago I attended a meeting in Louisville, Kentucky, with two dozen other pastors. It was supposed to be an annual meeting. In a matter of months two of the youngest and most vital among us would die, one of a malignant brain tumor, the other murdered by a burglar. We live as if we would live forever. At best, we don't live very long.

I am not trying to be morbid, but facing one's finitude is important, and it doesn't have to be morbid. It is simply realistic for me to know and admit that, like Moses, I will not live to finish everything. It is wisdom to accept that I will not experience everything.

Facing my mortality may help me practice a better stewardship of life. When I know I do not have an endless supply of something, I tend to become a better caretaker of it. I do not have an endless supply of days.

I am not suggesting that there is wisdom merely in knowing that I will die. Such knowledge alone may lead me to despair. It is important for me to have a Mount Nebo perspective informing my life. My living will be meaningful, not in the knowledge that it is limited, but to the degree that it is related to larger and longer realities.

The Spiritual Necessity

The earlier suggestion from Myron Madden that all of life is lived somewhere between Egypt and the Promised Land is as applicable to the inner promised land as to any other. As we turn from our orientation to external goals and undertake the inward journey, we should be clear that it is not a journey we will finish.

As Madden claimed, when we think we have arrived at the Promised Land, it always turns out to be more wilderness. This is true spiritually. The inward journey will not be finished in even the longest of human lifetimes. Consider St. Paul who, even toward the end of his life, at his time of greatest spiritual maturity, said:

> Not that I have already obtained this or have already reached the goal; but I press on to make it my own. . . . I do not consider that I have made it my own; but one thing I do: forgetting what lies behind and straining forward to what lies ahead, I press on toward the goal for the prize of the heavenly call of God in Christ Jesus. (Phil 3:12-14)

Browning's familiar lines from *Andrea del Sarto* say it best: "Ah, but a man's reach should exceed his grasp, or what's a heaven for?"

The spiritual necessity of seeing beyond my living, however, is not occasioned by my mortality but by my sin. The inward journey can become as egocentric as any outward journey. Just because it is inward, or spiritual, does not guarantee its purity or worthiness. We can be as self-involved spiritually as we can in any striving. Much New Age spirituality, for example, is totally narcissistic. For that matter, so is much contemporary Christianity. It may be a spiritual quest, but it can still be all about me.

Erik Erikson, in his brilliant work on psychosocial development, says that as adults we reach a stage where the alternative is "generativity" or "stagnation."[1] In other words, we come to a time when we decide whether we will invest ourselves in realities that will outlive us and find fulfillment, or whether we will remain preoccupied with ourselves in an infantile kind of self-centeredness and experience stagnation.

The journey toward the inner promised land, if it is to be redemptive, must at some point lose its way. I am not recommending wandering in the wilderness. Most of us have done enough of that. I am saying that the way of Jesus ultimately involves the losing of oneself. For many people this is the most enigmatic saying of Jesus: "For those who want to save their life will lose it, and those who lose their life for my sake will find it" (Matt 16:25). At certain points, even in the inward journey, I should find that my goals are becoming secondary to my concern for the horizons of others.

In a discussion by Peter Gomes of "the good life," I found a definition of happiness from Willa Cather: "That is happiness; to be dissolved into something complete and great."[2] This is the antithesis of our cultural definition of happiness, which seeks the enlargement and enhancement of one's own self and cannot imagine the self's dissolving as anything but a horror.

This infantile self-centeredness is the essence of sin. The longer we retain it, the more destructive it becomes, and the deep pool of the inner life becomes stagnant. Self-forgetfulness is the ultimate expression of love. Paradoxically, the more we lose ourselves in love, the more fulfilled we are. This, I believe, is at the heart of what Jesus meant when he called his followers to take up a cross. It looks like only loss, but it is inexpressable gain.

From Mount Nebo

What can we see from our Mount Nebos? If we see beyond our living, what is out there?

The Creator intends that children should outlive their parents. When this does not happen, it is a devastating tragedy. What we are giving those who will go on living when we are gone represent our most important investments. Of course I am not speaking only of our biological children, but of all those over whom we have influence. In what we give to others of love, of a sense of worth, of moral guidance, of vision, we are putting into the stream of history deposits that will still be there when we are forgotten. Unfortunately, the same is true of the negative things we give our children. We refer to the "important" people who "shape" history. The truth is, anyone who in any sense shapes a child shapes history.

Perhaps no generation has done as much for their young as we. We do everything for them, from seeing to it that they have their own rooms, wardrobes, cars, and computers to seeing to it that they don't miss a single cultural opportunity. We make our children's lives as pressured and frantic as our own. But what are we really giving them? What are we actually investing in their lives? Are we giving them an awareness that all of life is lived out before an eternal God? Are we giving them a sense of reverence for life? Are we helping them to know that life is moral to the core? Are we making the way of self-giving viable for them?

The problem is that we cannot give to our children, what we have lost or what we never received. But in our children we are seeing beyond our living.

We also see beyond our living in the church. I have a bias toward the church, not just the institutional church, which can become as corrupt as any institution, but the true church, the church as wherever people are living in the love and will of God, the church as the body of Christ. Don't junk the institutional church, however. It can serve as a framework for the true church, though it does not guarantee it.

Jesus said that the "gates of hell" will not prevail against the true church. The gates of hell will prevail against the civic club, the garden club, the country club, and both political parties. But whatever service we render *to* and *as* the church of Jesus Christ becomes a permanent part of the fabric of reality. Whatever we invest of ourselves in the true church, the kingdom of God, will live and serve and bless after we are long gone.

There is more for us to see beyond our living. It is more difficult to speak of than the ongoing lives of our children or of Christ's church. It is almost impossible to speak of this. We must, however, because it helps make sense of the rest.

In the Bible itself, the Promised Land always represents more than itself, more than just a geographical reality. The land Moses viewed from Mount Nebo was not an end in itself. Jews and Christians alike have seen the land, and particularly the city of Jerusalem, Zion, as a metaphor for the eternal realm.

However you conceive of it, heaven means the fulfillment of all things in God. Nothing makes much sense unless we can anticipate some completion or fulfillment. Even if we cannot conceive of it at all, it is important to believe in God's eternal realm.

Did you know that Moses puts in an appearance in the New Testament? He is not just referred to; he shows up. On the Mount of Transfiguration, with Jesus, appear Elijah and Moses. There is Moses, in the resplendent glory of the heavenly realm.

Moses was not permitted to enter the land because of a spiritual failure in his past. We do not know what that failure was exactly. But God didn't leave Moses in the mountains of Moab. God saw Moses all the way home. God saw him to the only Promised Land that matters, where failure need keep no one out.

Notes

[1]Erik Erikson, *Identity and the Life Cycle* (New York: International Universities Press, 1959).

[2]Peter J. Gomes, *The Good Book* (New York: William Morrow & Co., 1996) 197.